GLOBAL BEHAVIOURAL TRENDS

HISTORICAL EVOLUTION

AARKO

Contents

1. Introduction — 1

2. Colonial Mindset — 4

3. Britannia Rules The Waves — 7

4. Vive La France — 16

5. Small Island Syndrome — 21

6. Free Spirited Zeelanders — 23

7. Nippon — 28

8. Landlocked Lands — 34

9. Swiss — 36

10. Mongolia — 43

11. Afghanistan — 48

12. The Big Boy Syndrome — 53

13. Zhongguo — 56

14. The Land Down Under — 65

15. Canada — 71

16. Russia — 77

17. Yankees — 81

18. The Regional Satraps — 90

19. Singapura — 92

20. Deutschland — 96

21. Developing Nations — 101

22. Rainbow Nation — 103

23. Samba Country — 108

24. Rich Civilisations — 112

25. The Land Of The Pharoahs — 114

26. Persia — 116

Contents

27. Greece ... 122

28. Italy ... 128

29. Turks ... 136

30. Summary ... 140

CHAPTER ONE

Introduction

The global village that we inhabit is a cultural meltpot stemming from the diversity of its denizens. However, not surprisingly the focus of this diversity has always been on the physiological characteristics namely the colour of skin, type of eyes, hair texture, face structure etc. There are a variety of stereotypes associated with these overt traits that are tangible. Many of these are could be disgusting and downright racist. While the primary purpose of this book is not to examine this trait, it is also an important aspect which sculpts the behavioural aspect of a civilization. After all as Van Goethe said *"Behaviour is the mirror in which everyone shows their image."*

The books seeks to focus on the behaviour of a particular nation. The way one thinks, plans, reacts and engages with other cultures across the globe. This could be manifested in the form of whether the approach is friendly or cold; the level of trust and its deficit; conversational traits like calmness or aggression; circumscribing of behaviour based on any historical baggage with the recipient etc.

One of the key aspects of this behaviour is the degree of discrimination, also euphemistically known as racism. However, rather than an inherent one, it is a learnt behavioural trait influenced by the family and social milieu, education, media, culture etc. This is a trait that could clearly also be attributable to historical evolution of that nation.

Human nature and its diversity is such that racism is a quintessential part of human evolution. Equality which in a way in the anti-thesis of racism is a utopian concept. The question is not of whether it exists, but the degree to which it does so. Every civilization or human have some degree of racism inherent. The spectrum ranges from complete isolation like the apartheid era at one end to subtle ways of keeping out specific class of people even in vibrant democracies with strong institutions. It has been a thorn in the progress of a nation. Especially the distribution of economic gains has also been iniquitous on account of this trait. However, as Tim Wise had said, *"The very serious function of racism is distraction. It keeps you from focusing on the real issues."*

Some may argue that this is also a function of the physiological traits. The latter may be a function of what drives these behavioural traits. The entire concept of racism was manifested by the superiority complex that was built in by one race. It then used this to suppress the other culture. More important working on the psychological aspects of the latter. Infusing in them a notion that they were culturally inferior to the former. It was about breaking their will power to resist.

Another aspect of behaviour is the general approach of people. The way they conduct business or commercial transactions. The nature of their response and their attitude towards those from other nations. This is extremely important to understand so that one is prepared for eventualities and frame a suitable response.

Some of the smart traits that one expects during business negotiations are trust, integrity, patience, reading the others mind, building relationships, creating win-win situations etc. Roy Disney had said, *"Integrity is the most valuable and respected quality of a business leader."* Just like the discussion on racism, it is not a binary status of a trait like integrity being present or absent. It is about the degree of prevalence of it in a particular culture that we need to look at.

One way of looking at the genesis of all this is to dwell into the history of the country. This is a good barometer of the way of thinking and response to a different culture. It brings forth the core trait of a civilization and what to expect in any interaction.

However, one can argue that with the increased globalization, there has been waves of immigration. This has not only changed the demographic profile but brought with it various cultural nuances. It has significantly altered the core behavioral attitude of a nation. However, there is another school of thought that the immigrants themselves have been bigger adherents of the core cultural values than the original denizens. Why would this be? Maybe the fact that they are forced by circumstances to wear the sleeve of patriotism. Probably to show their newfound countrymen that they have completely given up their own cultures and assimilated into the country of their adoption. Hence, there could be circumstances that in interactions with the people of origin of another country, they might actually go out of the way to display the original traits of their adopted country.

Moreover, one must also understand that humans are diverse in nature. There is no *one size fit all* perspective of any culture. What can be found out is the broad perspective of these traits which are manifested in the basic nature of a culture. These characteristics are what determines the core traits of denizens of that country.

There is no doubt that these traits emerge when one looks at the history of these cultures. Therefore, a broad study of historical events, specifically the strategies used and the core motives provides a glimpse of the behaviour.

This book first looks at the history of some countries and then tries to infer about the global behavioural trends. Certain geographical aspects like that of being an island, a landlocked state or a large nation have also been looked at. These aspects also provide a perspective of the behaviour of some civilisations.

Hence, the aim is to gauge the general behavioural traits of a nation based on its history. This would be useful when interacting with such cultures. The last chapter provides the summary of how we need to interact with these nations across the negotiating table or even in a friendly banter in a café.

CHAPTER TWO

Colonial Mindset

The colonization of most parts of the world is part of the historical evolution of man. There were different motives for colonization ranging from trade to the need for more land for sustenance, slave labour and mineral resources. However, it was a period where oppression and exploitation were at its peak. While it was an era of economic genocide of the colonies, it enhanced the disparity of wealth and resources in these colonies. Foisting of external legal and administrative systems added to the complexity. The most pernicious was the psychological tool used of brainwashing the denizens of the colony of the inferiority of their culture and how they were being civilized in the colonial rule. To take the quote of Albert Memmi, *"The most serious blow suffered by the colonized is being removed from history and from the community. Their lands are confiscated, their ways of life destroyed, and all this is done in the name of civilization."*

Europe had been the hotbed of colonization. It was the explorers who initiated it but the funding was carried out by the monarchy or rich donors. Despite all the ills of colonization, one must give credit to the explorers who started off on their journey not knowing where they would land. While the journey to Asia was easier given the proximity to the lands that their ships traversed, it was the colonization of the Americas that was probably the toughest. Sailing across the vast Atlantic and Pacific Oceans not knowing what lay for them at the other end. Storms, rough seas that tested their vessels and inadequate stores and provisions for such journeys added to the degree of difficulty. Many, despite the work of the ancient Greek astronomers, were not absolutely sure whether the earth was spherical. Thus the question rose as to what would happen it they came to its edges. With such long journeys with no certainty of the destination, it was a ripe concoction for mutiny and rebellions.

These explorers however found new lands and then established trading posts there. Bit by bit, there were settlements which expanded these were in a way tantamount to land grabbing. As a result, they had skirmishes with the indigenous people who were defeated. These battles and the diseases that the explorers carried with them nearly drove the indigenous people to extinction. Moreover, they began to be confined to reserves.

The colonial mindset was one of commercial interest only. They extracted their pound of flesh from the colonies that they ruled over. They were economically impoverished as the wealth and resources such as precious metals made their way to the banking system of Europe. It was probably one of the darkest chapters of human history as many colonies which were the richest were impoverished beyond thinking.

Then there was the cultural genocide which led to the colonies actually been brainwashed into accepting the inferiority of their cultures. The language, education, economic structure was all altered to suit the needs of the colonisers and this had disastrous effects on the morale of those who were occupied. Their entire economic and political system was altered and the effect of this continues to this day in many of these colonies.

This was so much ingrained that even today there are many sympathisers of the colonial period. Some of them argue that the administration was efficient and they ran their colonies well unlike what the natives would have done. Another school of thought mentions the infrastructure development done by the colonizers while conveniently forgetting that all this was done to further their colonial exploitation objectives. There was not an iota of repentance or remorse over this period of exploitation and many have got away scott free. The famous quotation of Aime Cesaire comes to mind, *"Colonialism and imperialism have not yet settled their debt to us. When they have done so, they can judge us. We can then talk of gratitude."*

At the end of the day, the behavioural pattern of all these erstwhile colonial powers still reeks of the superiority complex that they have towards their erstwhile colonies. Some of the latter have even overtaken the GDP of the colonial power thereby carving a niche for themselves. Hence one can expect a condescending attitude towards the colonies. Racism would be manifested in the form of how they treat the citizens of these colonies.

Therefore, one can expect the crudest of behavior from these colonisers. Even today, they have refused to accept the economic and cultural development of their erstwhile colonies. Therefore, a possible response is to give it back to them in equal measure. They must be made to realise that one cannot carry the historical baggage and must look forward for mutual cooperation on an equal footing. Moreover, they are masters of their language with the gift of the gab. It is important that one must not fall into a trap as some of them can also sweet talk. Religion was also made a bedrock for putting the colonies off guard and then usurping their land. The famous statesman, Jomo Kenyatta had said of this strategy of the colonisers, *"When the missionaries arrived, the Africans had the land and the missionaries had the Bible. They taught how to pray with our eyes closed. When we opened them, they had the land and we had the Bible."*

We thus start with understanding the history of some of these colonial powers. The case of Britain and France have been taken since they were probably the greatest colonisers trying to carve out land among themselves.

****

CHAPTER THREE

Britannia Rules the Waves

The most prominent of colonisers was of course Britain. It is said that the *"sun never sets in the British Empire"*. How true even in the modern age as they control a number of islands across the three major oceans, the Atlantic, Indian and Pacific. However, it is this very history, colonial and pre, which shaped their modern day thinking. The very use of the term *"Great Britain"* also shows the arrogance that is written deep into the psyche as England sought to stamp its imprint on the globe with the union of Scotland and Wales.

It all began with England which was inhabited by the Celtics, also known as Britons and then by some Belgic tribes around the Iron age. Then the core of Britain became part of the Roman Empire in the early part of the last millenium. Subsequently came the Anglo Saxons who were basically Germanic tribes and introduced the old English. Then there were the Viking invasions from the Nordic region around 800 AD. The uniting of the Anglo Saxons around the 10th century led to the formation of the Kingdom of Britain.

The monarchy can be traced back to the Anglo Saxons who laid the foundation of the modern version with figures like Alfred the Great. The Normans established their dynasty in 1066 after which the House of Plantagenet came around in 1154 AD. There was a wave of antisemitism which led to the expulsion of Jews from the country in 1290. The Hundred Years wars pitted the country against France from 1337 to 1453. However, subsequent to this there were a series of civil wars with the most famous one being the War of the Roses after which the Tudor dynasty was established in 1485. Subsequently, the Stuart Dynasty took over. The Glorious Revolution occurred in this period and it was in the 16th century that Wales became part of Great Britain while Scotland was also subsumed in 1707. The modern constitutional monarchy came about with the Hanoverian dynasty in the 1700's.

However, the Industrial Revolution which occurred during the time of the Stuart dynasty laid the foundation stone for the colonial expansionism. However, it was trade that drove these colonial conquests and it was covertly done by trading companies like the East India Company who had their own armies. They negotiated hard with the monarchy to give them the rights to trade with India. With the colonial rule, a number of colonies came under the purview of the kingdom with India, the prized jewel, being part of it from 1857 onwards. The monarchy was the head of the British Kingdom controlling $1/4^{th}$ of the world area at its peak during 1921.

The royal family strangely owns most of the land holding in the country. This is through the Crown Estate which administers these land holdings and is managed through appointed Commissioners. It is said that this is not the private property of the royal head but remain with them till their reign. The revenues out of this vast land holding go to the Treasury for funding the civil services. A percentage goes back to the royal family too which is currently fixed at 12%. Since the revenues come out of the tax payer's money, it has become a bone of contention. The total worth of all these properties is more than £15 billion. The genesis of this ownership goes back to the Norman conquests wherein the king owned all the lands and then distributed it.

Despite the monarchy being designated as titular heads, they were relatively more powerful than the other kingdoms around the world. The British used them as a soft power in their geopolitical relations. They called it a diplomatic asset too. Hence, the monarchy was a mute spectator to the colonial rule that virtually sucked all the economic resources of its colonies and impoverished them. It was nothing short of an economic genocide.

The key role of the monarchy in the colonial rule was to grant charters to the trading companies like the East India Company. They also appointed governors and administrators to rule these far off lands. They were handpicked and often were responsible for the economic exploitation by extraction of resources. It was then followed by value addition in Britain and then selling the produce in these colonies. It was the classic way to drain the wealth of the colonies. The cities of Manchester grew up as a textile centre as they took the raw materials from India, processed it and sent it back to the colony for sale. Bipin Chandra the historian said, *"The Indian peasantry was systematically bled by the British government, and the resources of the country were mercilessly drained away to England."*

The monarchy was chiefly responsible for this. The royalty also provided the military forces to suppress any form of resistance from these colonies. Some of the commanders went overboard throwing all civility down the window as they used brute force to cow down any resistance. Some of these like the Jalianwala bagh massacre including of women and children in India was a testament to the brutality of the regime. On the cultural front, they were instrumental in spreading the British culture, language, religion and institutions. They also encouraged the settlement of Britishers in these lands.

Moreover, all the major colonial powers hide behind the veil of the atrocities committed by the Nazis in World War II. There is no doubt that the latter was pernicious in terms of carrying out atrocities but the colonial rule was no way better and led to the economic impoverishment of hitherto rich civilisations. They have peddled a narrative that the colonial rule was about civilizing and instilling the rule of law. What they forget is that it was a complete cultural and psychological indoctrination of the inhabitants that have left the scars to this date.

But their thought process as they went on the expansionist spree is one to be looked at. There was a method to their plan to overrun colonies with commerce being the factor. After all they were the original *"baniyas"* of the world, an Indian term used to describe traders. Hence, trade was the intoxicant which fuelled them to seek the shores of the sub-continent. Thus money was the only motive and could be had through any means.

Not surprising since India was the richest nation of the world despite the series of invasions until the mid1700. It was rich and accounted for 1/4th of the world GDP at that time, a drop from the 1/3rd global GDP figure during the end of the 1st millenium. The invasions during this intervening period were also pernicious for the economy. However, many of these invaders settled in the newly conquered lands and established empires. Thus it did not do the type of economic damage that the colonial powers did. The country was transformed into one of the poorest with probably nothing left to exploit further when the Britishers left its shores.

John Bright summed up the British rule in the country *"The British Parliament does not represent India, it represents only the English middle classes. The government of India is carried on for the profit of the English merchant and manufacturer."*

For the British, there was no better prey and it was no rocket science that the flotilla were directed to this oasis of wealth and prosperity. The other major economy, China had its own empire which was powerful and expansionist in intent. Thus the Brits did not want to risk an adventure there since they already had a soft target. Some of the other colonies like South Africa saw the rush for gold and diamonds which was another target for them.

While trading rights had been earned during the period of the Mughal Emperor Jahangir, the opportune time for them to strike was when this Indian empire was on its crutches due to infighting for succession. With all the other kingdoms split up, they used their pernicious divide and rule to enervate the country. The opposition fell like dominoes as they even ensured that the bigger kingdoms like the Marathas and Deccan kings did not form a coalition. The country was completely overrun by around the 1800-1850 with the princely states at the mercy of the Empire.

Behind the garb of the rule of law, they literally impoverished their colonies through deceit as well as the principle of divide and rule. Why was this so? Was it the small island syndrome wherein they sensed some insecurity and wanted to use all the wealth of the prized colonial possession to make them prosperous. Money was the only consideration and it could be got through any means. The colonies in the eastern hemisphere were the ideal targets for them to display all this wretchedness.

What happened was an economic disaster of a gargantuan proportion, with even the atrocities of the World Wars dwarfed in front of it. The west leaning historians, not surprisingly, overlooked all the inhuman side of this colonial rule. How could they cast aspersions on their forefathers who were the perpetrators of the biggest economic genocide the planet had ever witnessed.

Coupled with this, there were some economic disasters like the famines that ravaged much of the country. The poor were even further impoverished and many perished in these. There was no specific policy made to tackle droughts and the attendant famines that came with it. After all the colonial rulers were not there for providing governance but to plunder the wealth of the country.

The words of Winston Churchill sums up the British political attitude towards India which probably holds true for other colonies too, *"I hate Indians. They are a beastly people with a beastly religion. The famine was their own fault for breeding like rabbits."*

Never in the history of mankind had the richest country in the world been brought down to its knees and become the poorest nation in the world in a matter of a century. A record one would say looking at the rate of impoverishment. It is a barometer of the loot, plunder and rape of the one of the shining economies in the globe. Dadabhai Nauroji in his famous quote on the drain of India's resources said, *"The effect of this drain is to reduce the Indian population to extreme poverty. The annual drain of £30,000,000 is exactly equal to the entire land revenue of India. It means the drain of India's lifeblood."*

Famines and poverty bore its ugly head as the colonial rule was a calamitic disaster for its denizens. At the end of it all, what was left was not only the physical damage that the rulers brought forth but the emotional and mental scars that it left imprinted on the minds of many. These have still not been erased as the stories told down from generations have moulded the behaviour.

The next step was of course the strategy towards the denizens of the land. This was clearly enunciated through the process of cultural genocide that they perpetrated to brainwash the minds. The education system was tampered with and used as a pernicious means to tell young children about the system and how it was superior to their own. An inferiority complex was infused in them by peddling lies about their own culture and values. Young impressionable minds coupled with the defeatist attitude of their parents help sow in them the very thought process that the colonial power sought to.

The irony of it was that rulers peddled the narrative that they were civilizing the denizens and teaching them the rule of law. But what really occurred was a brainwashing that was steeped in lies and deceit. Even today, some people look back at those days as an oasis, probably convinced by the narrative which the generations had handed down to them. William Digby speaking on the colonial period said, *"The British claim to rule India for the good of the governed is a hollow sham. The British Empire in India is one long crime."*

The colonial rule of the British and other European powers were arguably the greatest crime in human history. They were stiff lipped and haughty justifying all these atrocities. Basically, they got away with murder as far as the sub-continent was concerned.

This clearly provides a perspective of the British thought process. For them it was about conquering lands through the principle of divide and rule. A game that they played smartly to outwit all the other kingdoms that were potential opposition. They amassed wealth and enervated their colonies sending them to a state of deprivation and poverty. It was nothing short of an economic genocide. Moreover, their media management of the entire colonial past was well masked as they hid behind the atrocities perpetrated by others like the Nazis. Even in the case of the other colonial powers, their shrewd tactics ensured that they remained in power.

The partition of India was also the handiwork of the colonial power. They created schisms in society as they propped up the religion card to divide and rule. With economic impoverishment, this was a good tool to create divisions and leave the colony in dire straits. The economic exploitation during the colonial rule was not enough. They needed to put a nail in the coffin of India and keep it cowed down and subservient to the colonial power. The Hindu-Muslim riots around the country during the partition left millions dead and the administration unable to check it. There is no doubt that those who left the shores after the end of their rule must have gloated in satisfaction at this heinous crime that they committed. If they wanted, the colonial rulers could have prevented the horrors of partition. Probably even kept the country united or even it they had to divide it, transfer power without the attendant genocide. This provides a good perspective of their thought process. Jawaharlal Nehru, the first prime minister of India summed up the British rule as, *"British rule in India was a monstrous system of exploitation, dehumanization, and suppression."*

Even in the post-colonial period, this policy was evident as they wanted to keep India weak. They foisted the problem of Kashmir as well as the boundary with Tibet which was left uncertain when they left the shores of India. Moreover, in the four wars that India fought with Pakistan and China, they clearly took a position against the colony they ruled. Even during the liberation of Bangladesh in 1971, they chose to ignore the genocide of the Bengalis at the hands of West Pakistan forces and instead sent a naval fleet to the Indian Ocean along with the Americans to ensure that India would not help the liberation. It was a different story that the presence of the Russians deterred both Britain and the US forces. All part of their psyche and thought process of ensuring that the colony should never progress even if they had to allow a large scale genocide elsewhere.

It's a different matter that the Indian economy finally grew larger that the colonial power in the 2020s thanks to the growing middle class and economic policies. The post Brexit scenario has created difficulties for the economy as they have been cut off from the supply chains of the European Union. This saw them trying to get into trade pacts with many countries including the colonies like India. Even in the trade negotiations with India during 2022-24, this attitude of a superiority complex is well evident. They have still not been able to come out of the colonial and baniya mindset. Some of the key traits evident in these negotiations are pontification, arrogance and the tendency to place money making above all principles.

The history of this nation can be summed up by the settlements and invasion by outsiders (Roman Empire, Germanic Tribes, Normans, Vikings etc). It was then followed by the setting up of the monarchy and the various houses or dynasty associated with it which had internal squabbles. Finally, in the attempt to seek lands in Europe, wars broke out with other powers like France. There was a phase of anti-semiticism too as Jews were driven out of the country. The Industrial Revolution was the trigger for the colonialization and the country was the most expansive with their navies sailing to all parts of the world. This period was the most ignominious one for the country but it is yet to apologise for all the economic crimes against the colonies. Therefore, the phase of external invasions, settlements, internal wars, fight with the French and the colonization was what has shaped the behaviour. It is primarily a trader's mentality with the smart policy of divide and rule with all their adversaries and colonies. The arrogance and haughtiness stems from the colonial domination and the belief that they can repeat those policies to subdue others.

As we sum up the British behavioural pattern, some of the key things are the following:

i. The basic mindset is that of a commercial trader and hence economic exploitation is at the crux of their thinking. This could manifest itself in foregoing all principles and focusing on extracting the moolah. As Michael Heseltine, a British politician said, *"The market has no morality."*

ii. Being the greatest colonial power at one point of time, they continue to look down upon their colonies in a disparaging way. They firmly believe that they are a superior race and this reflects in their attitude. This clearly has racist and discriminatory overtones.

iii. They are the masters of divide and rule. Having learnt this art during the colonial rule, they have carried this forward and would not mind experimenting it on others to achieve their ends.

iv. They put on the garb of sophistication and culture to get their stated objective. It is a means to put the other party off guard and then go for the kill. Therefore, this outward demeanour is a façade that must be cut through.

****

CHAPTER FOUR

Vive la France

The country sits as one of the key Members of the European Union. It has been flagbearer of the concepts of equality, fraternity and liberty, much of which was encapsulated in the French Revolution when the Republique was formed. The French are incredibly proud of this era and are immensely patriotic. Along with Britain, it was one of the great colonial powers that sent its explorers to all parts of the world. The colonial mindset is hence an intrinsic part of their thought process. The history of this country provides a perspective of the behavioural pattern of its people.

The region that is modern France was known as Gaul. It had an ethnicity of its own wherein the people spoke Gaulish. The region was conquered by the Romans beginning from the 2nd century BC until around 50 BC. Subsequently, the region was subject to a lot of barbarian raids and migration before being taken over by the Franks who were descendants of the Germanic tribes. While the region was united by King Clovis 1, it was Charlemagne, christened as the father of Europe, who ruled from 768 to 814 AD and made this region as part of his empire. Even the Pope recognized him as the ruler of Western Roman Empire. The region was known as West Francia. There was a line of succession but it witnessed the regional dukes and nobles exercising power. It finally went to the House of Capet which ruled under 1328.

However, there was a succession crisis after 1328 with the main protagonists being the Houses of Valais and Plantagenet. Another complexity that was brought about was the Hundred Years war in which the English tried to take over the powerful French kingdom, which was divided. One of the main characters during this time was the Joan of Arc, a peasant girl who led Valais to victory in 1453 over the English.

After succeeding to thwart the invaders, the Kingdom saw an absolute monarchy. It was also the period of renaissance and reformation which saw tremendous cultural and political progress in the region. However, there were further succession battles as the House of Valais was engaged in battles between the House of Bourbon and Guise.

However, it was Louis XIV's reign which saw the monarchy exert it most significant influence. He built up a strong military and was engaged in a number of wars including with the Spanish. The French kingdom became a force to be reckoned with during this period and set the stage for the subsequent economic prosperity through the industrial revolution.

However, a number of factors such as social inequality for land tenants, economic recession, food inflation, unemployment and a debt crisis let to a revolutionary uprising against the monarchy. The monarch Louis XVI considered reforms but domestic protests put paid to his plans. Finally, inspired by the American Revolution and the revolts in Europe, the revolutionaries who were primarily people across all walks of life, rose up in rebellion. The idea of equality, liberty and fraternity gained momentum and it led to the overthrow of the monarchy and the establishment of a Republic. The storming of the Bastille was the famous event encapsulated in this period.

However, the Republic had its birth pangs before Napolean established the French Empire. It was a phase of conquests and colonial France joined in the battle with other European powers to gain control of colonies. However, the defeat of Napolean led to further domestic angst as there were regime changes. It was vacillating between the monarchy and the various Republics. The last of them, the 3rd Republic was established in 1870.

The colonial history of the country is quite chequered. They also engaged in battles with the other colonial powers chiefly the Britishers, Dutch, Portuguese and the Spanish. While they went around to most continents of the world, what was stark about their rule as compared to the others was the imposition of French culture, chiefly its language. Of course, they economically drained their colonies which was the very purpose of undertaking the colonial conquests. Even today, this culture is prevalent in their colonies and the teaching of French is one such aspect. It has been so ingrained that some of the colonies actually fight more than the colonial power to preserve the language and culture. Vietnam was at the receiving end of their colonial rule and Ho Chi Minh has once said, *"For the people of Indochina, the most urgent task is to prepare for independence and the democratic republic, through resistance and struggle, because under French rule, the people suffer from both exploitation and oppression."* In the Indo-China front, the French were defeated by the North Vietnamese forces at Dien Bien Phu in 1954 which signalled the end of the French colonial rule in the region.

World War I saw the country with the Allied powers as they took on the might of the Germans. It resulted in the latter's defeat leading to the Treaty of Versailles signed in the country. While the interpretation of history may differ, it is the inequity of this treaty that laid the foundation stone for the next World War.

World War II literally exposed the French military as they were unable to put up a decent resistance. There were internal dissensions and the very pride of the French armed forces took a heavy toll. The Nazi juggernaut rolling over both fronts, the west and the east, in a time period that even the conquerors never expected. It was the capitulation of France in a few days that was the story of this war as the Germans tanks rolled into Paris. They installed the Vichy government in the south and concentrated their resources in the north. Ironically, during the initial phase, the resistance was also limited and many joined hands with the rulers. However, with the tide of the war changing due to the defeats of the Nazis on the eastern front, France played a crucial role in the internal resistance movement as it was liberated by the joint US and British forces.

After the war, the colonies were also liberated and the Republic got to grips with the post war restoration of the country. After all it had been economically drained on account of the Nazi occupation as well the fighting in its colonies in Indo-China and Algeria. However, the country became an important cog in the European Union wheel and has been piloting the Union along with Germany. It has been the cultural capital of the continent too, a legacy of the Renaissance movement.

To sum up the history of the country is one of the centre of invasions (Roman empire, Barbarians and Franks) before it became part of the Western Roman Empire under Charlemagne with a monarchy. There were internal strifes within its houses and a war with England which it managed to repulse. The monarchy became powerful but economic conditions led to a rebellion and establishment of a republic which the French are immensely proud of with the ideals of liberty, equality and fraternity. However, the period was not stable until Napolean embarked on his conquests which were also not successful as he had to retreat after entering Moscow. The French colonial rule fuelled by the industrial revolution and a mad scramble for colonies was pernicious in its intent. Africa, Canada and Indo-China were the main focus of the colonial rule. Somehow during the World Wars, they did not have the same firepower as some of the others and in the second World War capitulated in front of the Nazis. There is also an argument and the oppressors found many sympathisers of their regime and hence had a easy task. However, there was an internal resistance movement too which was a thorn in the flesh for the rulers. The behaviour is a function of this art of survival, clamour for freedom of speech and pride in the French language and culture.

As far as the behavioural aspects are concerned, there is the element of the denizens being a bit convoluted in the way they communicate. They don't believe in direct confrontation of issues.

Diplomacy has been a key aspect of the French interaction. They are, not surprisingly, proud of their culture and make it a point to spread it globally. The colonies ruled by them had this culture ingrained in them by the colonisers. Many of them, such as Francophone Africa actually seem more gung-ho than the French themselves to preserve the culture, chiefly the French language.

Therefore, in terms of expectations in any interaction, one must not expect straight talk. They are the masters of beating around the bush and trying to put one in a zone of comfort before getting to the core issue. No rocket science that they are wedded to their culture including the language. The socialistic genes are also seeped with the history of protests and revolution. Therefore, at the slightest provocation, they could be critical of things around and would provide their opinion. They have learnt the art of weaving through coalitions, both in their internal governance as well as in the EU. While they are economically powerful, the labour unions here are strong given the importance of rights. Hence one could always expect a lot of internal backlashes to policy changes.

On the business end, the French can be expected to show some patience. This is vindicated by the French saying, *"You can't make an omelette without breaking eggs"* or *"On ne fait pas d'omelette sans casser des oeufs"*. Moreover, it is also said that the French like to debate.

****

CHAPTER FIVE

Small Island Syndrome

A small island surrounded by water provides an entirely new physical dimension. The denizens of small islands carry a different outlook to life. Ensconced in a piece of land surrounded by a liquid mass, the thought process becomes a bit different from those inhabiting large land masses. Their behaviour is circumscribed by the fact that they are cocooned albeit separated from the mainland by a water body. How does this affect the thought process? Not easy to ascertain but the presence of a large neighbour across the mass of water definitely accentuates the fear.

It is not surprising that there exists this feeling of being looked down upon by a big brother across the straits. Even if there is no big brother, there could be other naval powers on the prowl and the history of colonization does not provide much comfort. These waters may act as a barrier but could also be perceived as a channel for any attack that may be mounted by the big adversary.

All this leads to a military thought process of building up a strong navy. But then with the size and resource constraints, it becomes one of mind games. This is where the element of mistrust germinates and behavioural patterns change. Then one may have to rely on a geo-political strategy of aligning with another powerful entity so as repulse any threats that might emanate.

Some of these islands literally stuck to the adage that *"attack is the best form of defence"*. Some like Britain and Japan were masters of this strategy and went on a military expansionist spree. Britain as indicated earlier had the largest colony. Despite the numbers not working in their favour, they recruited the locals into the military to tilt the balance.

Some believe that living in an environment surrounded by water could also influence one's thought process. It could become narrow and restrictive which could lead to a limited world view and resistance to new ideas. This may have to do with survival instincts. The limited knowledge can also translate into a lot of distrust and negativity to those outside. In certain cases, this can also germinate the idea of being culturally superior to others.

On the social front, it creates closer bonding among communities and even gives rise to the practice of sustainability. They are adaptive and resourceful enough to survive on the available resources. They are also proud of their cultural heritage and make all efforts to preserve it.

However, once again it is not prudent to ensconce all islanders in one silo. There are variations dependent on factors such as availability of natural resources, presence of large neighbours who could be threats, mode of settlement in the island etc. However, what one can say is that living in such an environment does influence the behaviour and thought process.

****

CHAPTER SIX

Free Spirited Zeelanders

Two large islands on the east coast of Australia with the vast expanse of the Pacific on its west. Its geographical location makes New Zealand fairly inaccessible. Hence its history is also quite new since there was no pre-historic habitation. With the isolation, there is a strong community bonding and the emphasis on self-reliance and resilience.

The Polynesians who are originally thought to have come from East Asia including the island of Taiwan began their journey across the unknown waters of the Pacific. The exploratory genes and bravado of these explorers with their primitive boats across unknown mass of water is nothing short of being incredible. They even went as far as Hawaii in the middle of the vast ocean. Samoa, Tonga, Marquesas, Easter Island, Society Island and finally New Zealand lay in their path. This is believed to have occurred in the period 1280-1320 AD as the explorers settled in these islands. Prior to this, all these islands are believed to have been uninhabited.

The descendants in New Zealand came to be known as the Maoris came during the period 1320-1350 AD in the last wave of settlements. Another group settled in the Chatham Islands in the east around 1500 AD and came to be known as the Moriori. Both of them developed their own unique culture. Maoris were primarily based on chieftainship with segregation of society.

Then came the European wave led by Abel Tasman, a Dutch explorer in 1642. Though he did not touch its shores, the naming of this country came from the Dutch region of Zeeland. In 1769, the

British explorer James Cook mapped out the country. In the series of explorations, the Britishers finally colonized the country.

The subsequent government undertook some reforms in the run up to the independence of the colony. There was extensive trade between the ships of US and European powers and the Maoris in the 1790s.

Christianity came to the country around 1815 AD through missionaries and spread to the indigenous people too. By 1845, nearly half of the Maoris were attending church services. The Europeans also began settling in these lands and this created a conflict of interest with the Maoris. This led to bitter confrontations.

The proliferation of European tools and weapons also imbalanced the internal power equations among the indigenous tribes. The musket was a potent weapon in wars and this led to many inter-necine wars wherein the party with this weapon easily overpowered the other tribes. Hence, everyone acquired these guns and this restored a semblance of balance of power. The attack on Chatham Island with these weapons almost drove the Morioris to extinction as a result.

The tension between the colonial powers and the indigenous people persisted during this period. Ironically, James Busby, a British Resident appointed by the crown encouraged the Maoris to sign a Declaration of Independence in which the rights of the land of the indigenous people was recognized. This was a phase of assertion of the rights of these people. Although the Crown agreed to this, they were not happy with this new power dynamics.

However, with the need of the colonial powers in the form of New Zealand Company to purchase land and in the light of the prevailing tensions, the Treaty of Waitangi was signed in February, 1840 with the Maori chiefs. The country became part of the British empire in May of that year. The Treaty was a classic case of legal obfuscation since there were different interpretations of its English and Maori version with the most pernicious being the powers of the British Crown to usurp Maori land in the English version with no such in the latter version.

However, the land disputes with the indigenous people persisted and this led to a series of wars. The presence of other European powers like France and Germany in these wars led to disastrous consequences for the Maoris as they lost their land with a foreign legal system imposed on them. Even the New Zealand government in 1877 virtually annulled the Treaty through a court judgment. It was one of the darkest phase of the indigenous people as their land rights were trampled upon.

The country was part of the Federation Council of Australasia from 1885 which included the self-governing colonies of Australia. It also participated in the Conferences of 1890 and 1891 leading up to the Federation of Australia. However, it refused to join the Commonwealth of Australia when it was formed in 1901 thus maintaining its self-governing status. Why did this happen? Some of the plausible reasons are the small island syndrome and the fear of domination by Australia. There were concerns on the economic isolation and limited say on trade with Britain and agriculture. National pride was a major factor and the skepticism on the role of big brother still prevails. Finally, the rights of the indigenous people like the Maoris was a concern since those in the mainland were on a different pedestal.

It became a self-governing dominion in 1907 and even joined the empire in the World Wars. Even during this phase, the rights of the indigenous people were trampled upon and this was probably a dark phase of their history.

With the passage of time, the Maoris began seeking greater rights and undertook protest movements. The Treaty of Waitangi became the basis of recognizing these rights and devolution of power in the governments of the 1950s and 1960s. The 1975 Treaty of Waitangi Act was the first attempt to recognize the Treaty through a Tribunal. However, there was a school of thought that this may have been too late since the land usurpation already occurred earlier and the Tribunal would not be able to undo all that. There have been other attempts for inclusivity with the preservation of the rights of the Maoris but it has not been an easy task.

While the relationship with Australia has by and large been conducive, there is a still a feeling of big brother. Not surprising, given the size and proximity to the large neighbour. The spirit of self-governance is manifested in this behaviour. One of the reasons as to why the country did not join the Federation was to preserve this unique culture and belief in self-reliance. All part of a small island mentality. Nevertheless, they have a close bonding with Australia in other areas such as celebration of ANZAC day when their joint forces fought in the World Wars.

How does the history of this land reflect in the behavioural pattern of the people? Basically, the history is of the colonization, uneasy relationship with the Maori and other indigenous people and finally the reluctance to be part of the Federation of Australia. All this leads to a mixture of the following traits. Despite the better relations with the indigenous people, a feeling of superiority given the fact that the Treat of Waitangi was not implemented in its spirit and all the usurpation of land already occurred before an effort was made to restore the balance of rights. Finally, the relationship with the bigger neighbour has largely been amicable but it is not surprising that the feeling of insecurity and inferiority creeps in. The history of the possible joining of the Australia federation which they refused plays a part in this.

So basically, one can expect them to have a tinge of racist behaviour but well masked behind the narrative that they treated their indigenous people better than the treatment meted out to the Aboriginals of Australia. They could take positions contrary to Australia in various forums given both the arrogance of the latter as well as a feeling of insecurity. Moreover, they have always believed in the concept of self-sustenance. This is clearly a reflection of the small island syndrome.

Finally, one does see traces of limited view of the world around them. Even with the flow of information in the digital age, it is about not really showing an interest in happenings around the world. This also manifests in an element of superiority complex over others. Sometimes, its blissful ignorance about matters beyond the island.

****

****

CHAPTER SEVEN

Nippon

Japan or Nippon is the land of the rising sun. The island country has been a centre of paradox over its history ranging from a spectrum of an isolationist policy to global integration as well as from a clan based system to parliamentary democracy. Arthur Golden had said about the country that *"Japan is a nation born of the meeting of the mind and the spirit. A society that recognizes beauty in the small, subtle, and simple things."*

Ancient history attributes to the presence of hunters gatherers around 40,000 years back. It was followed by the Jomon era from 13000 to 1000 BC where the inhabitants were also hunter gatherers but specialized in pottery. After the first wave of immigration from the mainland started with the Yaoyi era, the period saw rice cultivation, metallurgical advances in terms of weapons and tools, silk cultivation, weaving, woodworking, glassmaking etc. However, there was stratification of society and many tribes were constantly engaged in warfare.

After this came the Kofun era from 250- 540AD which saw attempts at unification of the country. The Yamato state in the central part was the hub around which this unification happened. The imperial dynasty was also established with the monarch at the head. It was also a period of interaction with both the Chinese and Korean kingdoms. The Asuka era from 540 to 730AD saw the Soga and Fujiwara clans establish. There were important developments in this era namely the introduction of Buddhism, christening of the country as Nihon, land reforms and administrative reforms.

The Nara period in the 8th century saw the publication of books as well as a series of natural disasters that shook the economy. The Heian era which lasted till 1185AD then saw clashes between the various clans as well as the deprivation of the powers of the imperial dynasty. However, it was a period of a cultural renaissance.

The Minamoto clan, which emerged victorious then started the Kamakura period in 1185AD by establishing a shogunate, who were the de-facto rulers with little role of the imperial court. However, with the death of Yoritomo, there were rebellions from the imperial house which was subjugated. With the help of the samurai, the invasion of Genghis Khan was repulsed but this weakened the shogunate after a rebellion let to their defeat. However, this was a period of agriculture prosperity due to the use of iron tools, fertiliser, double cropping and improved irrigation techniques. This period lasted till 1333 AD.

The next era was the Muromachi which went on till 1568 AD. The samurai installed a rival royal family thus leading to the division of the Court. Moreover, there were challenges from the daimyo or governors and ninjas who were spies hired by the former. The country then went into a civil war and broke down into various regions. It was in this period that the Portuguese came to Japan in 1543 for trading. They also got involved in the power struggle of the daimyos and provided arms and ships for the same. Christianity also spread around the country during this period on account of the Jesuits. This era also saw the development of currency trading and arts such as ikebana, bonsai, tea ceremony etc. Finally during the latter half of the 16th century, the shogunates managed to unite the country after bitter wars. There were even attempts to invade China and Korea but these were not successful.

The Edo period of the Takugawa shogunate from 1600 to 1868 was perhaps the longest period of stability in Japan. They managed to unite the country and more importantly kept a tight leash on the daimyos. They were the first ones to have harsh penalties for crimes which also instilled law and order in society. Christianity was clamped down upon and a completely isolationist or sakoku policy was adopted including preventing people from travelling. Most European trading rights were curbed and only Chinese, Koreans and the Dutch were granted these rights. During this period, culture and entertainment forms flourished, literacy levels rose while the four-tier social stratification of society occurred. However, the fall of this shogunate was instigated by internal rebellion of the samurai and peasants as well as the entry of the United States with its gunboats. However, this was undoubtedly the phase when the seeds of inward looking and the distrust of foreigners seeped into the genes.

The monarchy was reinvigorated after the collapse of the shogunate in 1868 with the ascendancy of Emperor Meiji starting off the era named after him. Sweeping reforms were undertaken like removal of the social class structure and ban on Christianity, tax reforms, infrastructure development, dispersion of scientific knowledge, formation of government institutions and creation of a patriotic nationalism through Shintoism as the official religion. This was the era of expansion of the Japanese army fuelled by the samurai in the Meiji regime. It was premised on the notion of the need to have colonies with a skirmish with the Taiwan setting the tone. They defeated the Qing dynasty of China in 1894 and the Russians in 1905 setting the stage for their imperialistic ambitions. A military alliance was also signed with the British in 1902. The annexation of Korea was completed in 1910. The industrialization of country also occurred chiefly with the growth of family run businesses called zaibatsus like Mitsubishi and Sumitomo.

During the regime of the next Emperor Tasho until 1926, greater political freedom was granted with manifestations of protests and riots including on rice. During World War 1, Japan was with the allies and got the South Pacific colonies of Germany. While the stature of Japan grew internationally due to the war, there were some dark spots like the Kanto massacre of Koreans.

Emperor Hirohito then ascended the throne in 1926 and was the longest monarch until 1989. This was the phase where extreme right wing nationalism took roots in a sinister form. The war with

China was instigated by an internally planned attack on a Manchurian railroad. The Kwantung army used this as a pretext to occupy Manchuria. Moreover, the Japanese army became powerful and took control over the political establishment in the run up to World War II, aided by the image of the politicians being corrupt. With this powerful military and the policy of expanding territories, the Japanese army launched an offensive on China in 1937 and captured the major cities like Beijing and Shanghai. They also carried out a lot of atrocities on civilians.

The country also made significant progress in science and technology. However, this was primarily to make a strong military. Albert Einstein had said, *"The Japanese mind, with its high sense of beauty and simplicity, is peculiarly suited to the work of the scientist."*

It was the US sanctions at this point of time that drove Japan to align with Germany and Italy in WW2. They invaded East Asia quite successfully coming up all the way to the North eastern part of India. Once against the country came up for a lot of flak due to the atrocities committed on the occupied areas with tales of torture and gross human right violations.

The bombing of Pearl Harbour was probably the turning point of this war as the US that had been a bystander entered the war. With the change in the tide of the war, Japan lost these captured territories to the Allies chiefly the US. The major losses were in the Battle of Okinawa including the sinking of the warship Yamato. Finally, rather than launching a full scale land invasion to subdue the stubborn Japanese resistance, the US chose to test its atomic bombs on Hiroshima and subsequently Nagasaki in 1945. That was what brought the country to its knees and made it surrender.

The post war Japanese governments have become close to the US and the west. With the type of discipline that the Japanese have, it made the country prosperous raising the standards of living. It even made apologies about its war crimes though the countries on which this was perpetrated like China and Korea have not fully accepted this.

How has their behaviour been moulded by history? With the clan based system, the society has evolved into an effective and consensus based decision maker. However, the inward looking policies of the Takugawa shogunate was what instilled in the suspicion of foreigners and made them racist. This got reflected in the colonial rule where they subjected their colonies to atrocities of a scale higher than that of the Europeans. Nevertheless, their reign was too short to have the type of economic genocide that the European colonizers subjected the colonies to.

Finally, coming to the behavioral aspect, it is a strange set. On the one hand, they are disciplined, hard working and good team players. But the discipline sometimes get overstretched and the society has tremendous mental health issues including high suicide rates. However, the colonial rule over the South East and East Asian countries and the war crimes brought out their true nature, cruel and arrogant. Therefore, racism percolates deep in the psyche and is visible. Even today, they internalize that they are a superior race atleast in Asia. Another aspect is the status of women. It is a strange concoction that despite being a developed country, women hardly hold positions of power in society. Virtually in all streams of life including politics, they are hardly represented and social norms have kept them subdued.

So what can one expect from the average citizen of the country? One very distinct one is the feeling of racial superiority. However, they are pragmatic and after tasting defeat in the war have managed to restore the economic powerhouse status of the country. This shows that they are disciplined and hardworking. They are especially good in team work and have learnt to take orders from superiors with little show of dissent. In line with their brief colonial period, the tag of being cruel and inhuman would remain with them especially when compared to the European colonial powers. They are slow in the decision making and would not take a call unless they have done their homework and are absolutely sure.

On the other aspects, there are some facets of Japanese culture which are critical to understand. They are respectful with traits such as bowing, polite language and deference to superiors and elderly. Moreover, they are polite and humble in their dealings. Punctuality is a key trait and it is important to be on time in their meetings. The concept of loyalty to family, society and enterprises is also an important aspect. It makes a sense of belonging and encourages teamwork. Finally, they do not confront issues upfront and avoid situations of conflict. They are good resolvers trying to work out compromises.

****

CHAPTER EIGHT

Landlocked lands

The landlocked lands probably had a different approach in terms of their interactions with the outside world. The basic premise for them was that they were surrounded by nations, potential adversaries, from all sides and there was no option to have navies which would have satiated any expansionist desires. However, this also creates a strong cultural bond among its citizens. As Peter Maurer said, *"Landlocked countries often have a profound sense of isolation, but they also have a deep resilience and a unique cultural identity forged by their circumstances."*

It creates a scenario of always being wary of the intent of the country across the border. Yet one probably has to depend on them for a variety of economic needs. Therefore, it was a matter of either maintaining good relations along these borders or overwhelming them. Moreover, since trade and commerce had to occur through these land routes, maintaining peace was vital. It was also susceptible to attacks, the most dangerous of these being multi-pronged ones.

This sense of insecurity is what drives the thought process of many of these nations. *"Most bad behaviour comes from insecurity"*, said Debra Winger. It is precisely this feeling of susceptibility that drives the strategy of these nations.

One of the strategies used is to pit one adversary against the other. This is in case of buffer states ensconced between two or more large players. All of these protagonists eyeing the prized catch sitting across their border. One might think that this is a devious strategy but then in many cases, it is a matter of survival and this could be the only option.

Then of course, there are players who believe that probably one would need to be adventurous. Maybe even taking on the adversary in their moment of internal political or military weakness. The tactics could also be different and not be a conventional warfare. Akin to the hit and run or guerilla tactics that make up for the imbalance as far as the prowess or efficiency of the military forces are concerned.

All these strategies need to be rightly concocted to keep the adversaries guessing about the next move. This calls for developing a mindset of suspicion and reading too deeply into every move that is made. Strengthening the military has been one of the key elements since it is all about defending the land borders which are susceptible to being breached.

The overall behaviour was of course crafted as an amalgamation of all such factors. Realpolitik was the name of the game and it was important to have a strategy that would ensure their survival. History is witness to the multitude of approaches made by various countries caught in the web of being landlocked. Some even tasted success in carving out some of the biggest empires in history while others just buckled under the pressure mounted by those around them. But one thing is certain, many have learnt the art of playing realpolitik in the game of survival.

****

CHAPTER NINE

Swiss

Switzerland is a haven for tourists. The Alps and the Juras provide some spectacular views even though they dwarf in comparison to the Himalayan peaks. There are mountain lakes, meandering rivers, slow moving glaciers, undulating meadows and thick forest cover that add to the splendour of this place. The bucolic beauty is well preserved and prosperity is all around for one to see.

However, beneath this veneer of affluence lies a history that saw a lot of trial and tribulations. One marred by a lot of invasions, internecine strife and a cat and mouse game with the potential adversaries. Something which enabled the cantons to survive and flourish. This instinct of self-survival is what the denizens of this land carried with them. A landlocked nation that had to weather the adversities, not merely by force but by their smart maneuvers' and presence of mind.

The history began with the settlement of a number of Celtic tribes including the Helvetti. The Roman era began in 58BC under Julius Ceasar when these tribes were defeated. Roman culture thrived during this period and one can see a number of architectural marvels even today. With the fall of the empire, it was invaded by Germanic tribes and was part of the Frankish empire under Charlemagne.

Under the Holy Roman Empire during the 10th century, the country had independent states known as the Cantons which was the genesis of this modern nation. It all began with the three original cantons of Uri, Schywz and Unterwalden in 1291 which were joined by others. It was a means of countering external threats. Circumstances forced some of them to come together to form the Early Confederation. They were in a way independent in terms of their currency, army and administration.

The first real tryst of these early confederations was a war with the Habsburg dynasty in Austria where they were victorious in the 1387 Battle of Sempach. This victory despite the numbers not supporting them catapulted them into prominence. They became powerful and in this period even created the Swiss mercenaries who were a group of battle hardened fighters. The other kingdoms were in a way outsourcing these mercenaries for their wars. This was a smart move since it not only got them the moolah but helped them create a strong force for themselves. Being cocooned amidst all the empires taught them this strategy of self-survival.

There were internal conflicts along religious lines too with Protestant reform movements of Zwingli and Calvin during the 16th century. The Peace of Westphalia in 1648 was a treaty that ensured Swiss independence from the Holy Roman empire. The next test came with the French empire overrunning them in early 1800 but independence was restored within 15 years. With the limited French rule, not much changed.

The country's cantons were a mixture of four languages, three of these being German, French and Italian. The fourth was the ancient language of Romanche. The cantons came together with pressure from all fronts like the Duke of Milan, Prussian Empire and the French Empire. They had to navigate very cautiously and used the tactic of playing one against the other well. Something akin to the divide and rule strategy of the British. The supply of mercenaries to these parties was a good move in order to get the moolah and ensure safety from any military intervention.

A civil war in 1847 was along religious lines but in the aftermath the confederation was restored. This was a difficult period since the cantons fought among themselves but the victors understood the importance of retention of the confederation to survive.

The acid test however came during the World Wars, especially the second one. An Independent Commission of Experts (ICE) presented its report in 2002 on the role of the country in the World War II. This was the first admission of the role of the country during this global conflict and how it profiteered despite being a so called neutral party. It was probably the country which benefited the most from this conflict as both the Parties to the actual war went into an economic recession and had to resuscitate their economies.

The Confederation which was a mixture of French, German and Italian speaking population thus had mixed support in both the wars. The Central and Entente Powers in World War 1 as well as the Allies and Axis powers in World War II. Language was a key factor since Germany, France and Italy were part of one of these groups. Yet they smartly managed to keep the dissent under check. They also built a military which was ready to take on the potential aggressors. Through the Confederation had built up a reputation as far as their military was concerned, they really did not stand much of a chance if they had to take on the firepower. The terrain of the Alps and the Jura would have been a potent natural defence. It could have a war of attrition and probably this was a factor too in obviating any aggressive intent. A lot of refuges of the war also trickled into the country.

The real weapon was however the moolah. The country was a major financial centre They managed to keep the money of both the sides, more so the Axis powers in World War II in their banks. This was used as a strategy to prevent themselves being overrun by the Axis. In way, this was a crime since it was the tainted money used to fund wars and the genocides within it. It was a well kept secret as the country was a police state and could control information. The other nations in the European mainland were aware of this and carry resentment to this date.

The country was also the primary exchange for the Nazi gold that was stored in its vaults. It was also the main clearing house for the precious metal. Much of this gold was stolen from the victims and parked in Switzerland since it was considered a safe haven. It is believed as per a report that 77% of gold deliveries of the German central bank were handled in Swiss banks. More than 90% of these volumes were done by the Swiss central bank itself. The total commissions received by the central bank were to the tune of 1.7 billion swiss francs.

The country was also a major supplier of arms and ammunition to both sides. During World War II, in the pre-war years, bulk of the supplies were made to France and United Kingdom. The Confederation was thus supporting the Allied powers and saw an opportunity to make money in the lucrative arms exports market. However, with German pressure as the war began, they switched sides and started supplying the Nazis with the state of the art weapons. As per the ICE report, a number of companies such as *Dixi, Hispano Suiza, Oerlikon Bührle, and Waffenfabrik Solothurn* began focusing on the lucrative export market.

The concept of neutrality in the war was a hoax perpetuated to keep a clean image. There is no neutrality in a war like situation. Unless you appease the parties through whatever means money or arms, you can never be expected to be out of the war zone. The Swiss played their cards smartly, supplying their mercenaries, being a safe haven for the money and gold of these powers, supplying arms and ammunition .

The Axis powers chiefly the Nazis did threaten but the confederation used all tactics, military, humanitarian and economic to prevent it. As the war waged on and the Axis were defeated, this was a win-win situation as the Swiss confiscated all the money and gold. So the banking system was flush with funds, all ill gotten and tainted. In a way, without putting any foot on the battleground, they were the chief beneficiaries in the conflict making a lot of wealth and not having any of their territory occupied. They literally laughed their way to the bank and mocked the adversaries on both sides of the battle who were licking their wounds and trying to build up their battered economies from scratch.

Subsequently too, it became a haven for all the ill gotten wealth of dictators and high net worth individuals being parked. There were instances when these dictators were overthrown and no one to claim the money. In those cases, it was obvious who got this wealth. There was a safety aspect to this as the country was considered neutral. It smartly defended its borders and did not involve itself in any global conflict.

Another case where the Swiss deserve credit is the mushrooming of a number of international organisations in Geneva. On the garb of being neutral, they have been able to market the country as the ideal location to discuss geopolitical tensions. Thus international organisations like the United Nations (UN), World Trade Organisation (WTO), World Intellectual Property Organisation (WIPO), World Meteorological Organisation (WMO) etc. It is a long list of such organization which are based on the western most point of the country in Geneva. This has also ensured enough flow of money through the presence of so many diplomats in this place. It has created a huge flow of wealth as people travel for meetings of these organization throughout the year at a regular frequency. Whether there is any utility of any value addition is totally immaterial. It is a self-fulfilling prophecy since all the Members love to travel to the beautiful country and there is inertia to alter this status quo.

One solid example is of the World Economic Forum (WEF). This is actually an annual rich man's party in a Swiss village of Davos known more for skiing. The who's who of politicians and corporates descend into its narrow alleyed village roads and it completely transforms Davos. The hospitality sector of the village pockets most of this money. The WEF, started in 1971 as an inter-governmental organisation, is based, not surprisingly, in another Swiss town of Geneva. Founded by Klaus Schwab, it was a forum for getting government, business and academia on a common platform to shape their agendas. It began as a forum for European business to learn from the practices in the US. However, slowly the animal grew to encompass all major global players. The annual meeting in Davos and regional conferences elsewhere generate a lot of revenue. However, its overall utility is still under a cloud. There are murmurs of its capturing of global institutions, taxpayers money being spent, tax exempt status of WEF, lack of clear processes and transparency and the environmental footprint in this remote Swiss village. None of the participants would openly admit the latter since why should they stop their annual vacation being held at someone else's expenses. Why should one kill the goose laying golden eggs for them?

The stashing of the money of various regimes around the world like the Nazis, Gaddafi regime of Libya, Emirs of the Middle East and many others shows their shrewdness. This brought them peace with the Nazis who did not invade the country during World War II. Finally, when the regime was defeated it was a double whammy as they pocketed all the money. They have created a halo of the country being neutral and hence a safe haven for stashing ill gotten wealth.

Thus the Swiss are a classic example of a shrewd tactic for survival. Surrounded by adversaries all around, they mastered the art of how to become useful for them, either through supplying mercenaries, or arms and finally being safe havens for their money and wealth. They build up a defence mechanism in case of any conflict and managed to survive all the trials and tribulations. There were literally no principles and as long as someone had money, they would befriend them. To put in it one terse phrase, it would not only survive but use the opportunity to thrive.

The twenty six cantons of the country personify democratic institutions. They have significant autonomy which allows them to make their own laws provided they do not contravene the Federal laws. There is direct voting on many issues through referendums and initiatives. The system is unique to the country and has developed over many centuries. Peter Conoway, a US Ambassador to the country has stated that it is *"A successful but frequently frustrating alpine democracy"*.

What has history taught them in the evolution of their behaviour? The repeated invasions (Germanics, Franks, Romans, Habsburg, French etc) taught them the art of both defending and having key allies. Towards the modern era, parking of money and supply of mercenaries was used a key instrument in this tactic. Finally, they have played the economic card smartly to encash upon the tourism, financial services and niche product sectors.

So what can one expect from them in terms of behaviour. They are smart businessmen and so one can expect them to be good dealmakers. The racist tendencies definitely exist given that they even consider other European countries such as those from EU a notch below their stature. There is no wonder that they have managed to keep the place spic and span with all amenities that are conducive for flourishing of tourism which is a major of revenue. Diplomatic tourism is also one of their fortes as most international organisations are based out of Geneva. In the name of the tourist moolah, the racist behaviour is well masked. However, since money is the key driver, expect them to go to any extent to earn it.

****

CHAPTER TEN

Mongolia

Mongolia has been historically associated with the Mongol empire and its enigmatic leader Genghis Khan. He along with Alexander the Great is supposed to have carved out the largest empires in world history through conquests. But behind the veil of this great Mongol warrior lies the strife and struggle that this land had to endure. It is landlocked and the climatic conditions are not so conducive for human habitation chiefly due to the arid expanse of the Gobi desert.

Lying between the two great expansionist empires of China and Russia, it witnessed constant wars for its very existence. The only option was to take the support of one to prevent the other from invading. This dilemma is well reflected in a Mongolian proverb that goes, *"To be without a friend is to be poor indeed; a nation with neighbours is isolated indeed."*

The presence of horses, that were the only means of fast transport in these grasslands, gave them an advantage. But beyond these horses, there was something in the Mongol genes that made them search out in conquest of new lands. Even the Tian Dynasty of the 1700's which was the basis of Chinese expansionism, was founded by the Manchu bannerman riding on the horses, who could be traced back to Mongol blood in the Manchurian region. It is a different matter that they got in diversity into their regime by having personnel of other origin like the Han Chinese.

Historically, it was a land of nomads with various tribes inhabiting it. Vast open plains, a cold and dry desert with patches of vegetation and little source of water. Nomadic life was the only option and even till this day, very little has changed as far as the rural communities are concerned. Therefore, this way of life had ingrained in them the need to expand for tapping in more sources of water and food. Animals were the primary source of nourishment both in terms of meat and milk. Very hard conditions making the horse the lifeline for many of them.

Some of the dynasties that came to establish themselves in this place were the Xiongnu which came around the 3rd century BC to around 1st century AD. While they expanded, they were defeated by the Han dynasty of China. Subsequently, there was the Xianbei dynasty, comprising of people of Donghu origin which existed for another 150 years. They too were nomadic but not as well organized as the Xiongnu. Subsequently, there was the rise of the Rouran Khaganate who were also of Donghu origin. There are many theories about them including that they were the first to have chiefdoms, had a aggressive military strategy and were also stated to be "*a band of Steppe robbers*" as they extorted from people using the region for trade. Many theories say that the Tartars originated from them and they also settled in the Byzantine empire in modern day Hungary.

This was followed by the First and Second Turkic Khaganates. They stretched their empires from modern Turkey in the west to parts of southern Russia too. However, it was at war with the Tang dynasty of China, and losing battles to the latter. After the fall of the Tangs, the Liao dynasty took control of this area from 916 to 1125 AD and expanded its influence. They too continued their expansionism with the Song dynasty. Eventually, they lost to the Jin dynasty and got assimilated into the Mongol Empire.

The high point of this region was of course the Mongol Empire which began by uniting the Mongol tribes in 1206. Genghis Khan was one of the greatest emperors as he expanded his empire right from the sea of Japan to Eastern Europe. The north-south expanse stretched from parts of the Arctic and present day Scandinavia to India and China. He undertook some major reforms such as subdivisions of the army, a new code law, record keeping, religious freedom, literacy, adaptation of the Uyghur script etc. It was the bedrock of the empire which expanded after his death too. It was the greatest expansion in human history, the pinnacle of the history of the region. The empire was divided into different Khaganates based on the geographical region they operated from. Of course, subsequently, there would be further divisions and disintegration of the empire with succession becoming an issue.

Subsequently, the Yuan dynasty took over the region as it was a successor state to the Empire. It had retained some of the territories in China too. However, with time, they were forced to go back to the Mongolian plateau as they lost the southern parts to the Ming dynasty. However, they were the first non-Han rulers of China. However, the Yuans were eventually defeated by the Qing dynasty who took control of the region at the end of the 17th century. This was the only time in the history of the Mongols that they were under a foreign power for a long period of time. However, it was not a one way street since they managed to retain a lot of autonomy.

One of the interesting facets was the fact that Buddhism had come to spread in the region primarily due to the influence of the schools around. One of the Mongol Khagnates had raided Tibet in the 1500's. They managed to force the supreme monks to surrender. In one of the tacit agreements with the Gelug School of Tibetan Buddhism from which the Dalai Lamas come, they recognized the latter's post. The Gelug School thus dominated over the other schools in Tibet due to this recognition. Buddhism spread in Mongolia during this time. This is a pointer to the fact that the civilization was more inclusive in its approach towards other religions.

With the Chinese revolution of 1911, Mongolia declared its independence from the China imperial dynasties. Nevertheless, it was not easy as the Chinese Republic was engaged in a battle of attrition to dominate. However, it was during this period that the Russian influence over the region became predominant. While the Chinese took advantage of the Russian revolution to capture the region, ironically it was the Russian white guards to came to the rescue by defeating the Chinese forces. Baron Ungern who was head of the Russian troops allied with the Mongolian monarch Bogd Khan. His aim was to get allies in the fight against the Soviets. However, at this time the Mongolian People's Party (MPP) was also formed and the Soviets aligned with that. In the ensuring struggle to protect Mongolia from China, Baron Ungern was also captured in the assault on the capital Urga. The formal independence was got only in 1921.

However, post independence, the influence of the Soviet Communist party was predominant since they had played a critical part in the independence of Mongolia. The communist system also became part of the political landscape of the country and it was geo-politically aligned to the Soviets. With perestroika, things changed. It was only during the 1989 revolution that the country became a democracy with a new constitution in 1992.

The learning from the history of Mongolia is that the landlocked nature of the country and the terrain made it susceptible to outside invasions. Therefore, its rulers had the ingrained idea of attack being the best form of defence. Even before the great empire, the rulers were constantly on the lookout for expanding their territories. However, the succession wars was what put paid to the ambitions. Even the Great Empire could not be sustained due to this and had to break up into Khaganates. Finally, the divisions showed up and the small kingdoms could not resist the pressure from the Chinese dynasties and fell prey to the Tang dynasty that overran them. However, they managed to hold their own in the struggle for independence and the presence of the Soviets bailed them out. A buffer state between the mighty Chinese and the Soviets worked for them.

When one looks at the behavioural aspects, there are some strands that come out clearly. The conditions of the cold and dry desert made these people strong within since it was a matter of survival. The horsemen that they were came to their advantage as they could roam around the Steppes on horseback and conquer lands. The Great Empire brought about the sense of planning and rule of law that saw the clans being united and being a force to be reckoned with. They managed to hold their own for much of their history before falling prey to the Qing dynasty. However, the strong fighting power in them enabled them to escape from being in the clutches of the latter as they took the help of the Soviets. So one can sum up the denizens of Mongolia into strong, sturdy and exploratory in nature. The fact they had close relations with the Christians, Buddhists and other Islamic sects shows their willingness to have an inclusive culture. There is a saying that, *"The Mongolian steppe nurtures a spirit of freedom that few can understand, and even fewer can conquer."*

****

CHAPTER ELEVEN

Afghanistan

A country, now often associated with violence and fundamentalism was once ironically the centre of spiritual thought. Buddhism, Hinduism, Islam and Zorastrianism flourished in its valleys and the land had been relatively peaceful. Landlocked with the Hindukush and Pamir ranges straddling through, it has a dry terrain with difficult conditions for habitation. The valleys are the only oasis for life around which settlements have emerged.

It was however, the epicentre of a number of external aggressions as also the route to trade with the sub-continent. The Silk Road passed through it and hence its strategic location was what made it a prized possession for the invaders. It all started with the Persian empire which repeatedly tried to occupy it. Alexander the Great had overrun it during the expansion of the Greek empire in around the 4th century BC. He is believed to have said of the Afghans that, *"I am involved in the land of a brave and noble people."*

It was also attacked by the Mongols, Mauryan empire and the Arabs. Modern Afghanistan was a buffer between the Russian empire and the British colonial rulers. However, both of them attempted to conquer it to thwart the efforts of the other. Finally, it became the hotbed for the cold war dispute as the Soviets and Americans made it their battlefield. The country was caught in this vicious cycle and saw its maximum destruction during this period as the two superpowers tried to control it.

Historically, it was Ahmed Shah Durrani who is considered the first emperor to unite the nation. He went by the last name of

Abdali, from the name of his tribe. He defeated the Marathas in the famous 3rd battle of Panipat in 1761. However, he returned after this victory due to succession battles and did not seek to expand the empire into the sub-continent. On his return journey, he lost a lot of men primarily due to the guerrilla warfare tactics. The succession battle led to the fragmentation of the country and a civil war. It was only in the middle 19th century through the war of unifications that Dost Mohammed Khan made the modern state. However, his death once again threw the country into chaos. It then became the battleground in the war between the Russians and Britishers.

The British colonial power waged three battles against the Afghans. They were repulsed in the first battle but managed to win the second one. This was how the British influence was established in the country. Nevertheless, in the third war, they tasted defeat and were chased out of the country with Amanullah Khan establishing monarchy in 1926.

This monarchy lasted until 1973 and was a period of liberal views in the country. A land very different and more inclusive than what it is at present. Subsequently there was a coup against the monarch Zahir Shah orchestrated by his cousin Daoud Khan. The Republic of Afghanistan was thus established but little action happened on the reforms promised. Hence the government was deposed in a military coup in 1978 by the People's Democratic Party. This established a communist regime with support of the Soviets. The secular policies coupled with the repression of the religious heads and intelligentsia and the external support created some internal strife. The Soviets had to intervene militarily in the end of 1979 due to the unrest across most provinces and they occupied the country.

With such a geo-political shift, the Americans began their support of the Mujahideen to fight the communist regime. This was a group of trained militia whose aim was to oppose the ruling party and the Soviets. The Americans did the funding through the ISI, the intelligence agency in Pakistan. However, this was the genie that the Americans uncorked which would go out of their control and eventually lead to the creation of forces like the Al Qaeida which came back to haunt them. With entrenched fighting that was proving to be expensive for the Soviets, they had to withdraw in 1989.

The Soviet installed a regime led by Najibullah and he was captured and murdered by the Mujahideen in 1992. However, the latter could not wrest control of the country since there were other factions too. Ahmed Shah Masood was based out of Panjsher valley near Kabul and he captured the capital before the US funded militia could. There were other warlords like Gulbuddin Hekmatyar and Rashid Dostum too who were part of the power struggle in the country. The Iranian backed Hezb-I-Wahdat was also one of the protagonists in this power struggle. Burhuddin Rabbani became the President in the country. He had the support of the Pakistan intelligence ISI who wanted to have their sphere of influence in the country. Thus it was a complex and vicious fiefdoms at loggerheads with each other.

A city called Kandahar was at the centre of this struggle between many tribes. The ground was fertile for the creation of a new group known as the Taliban. The group owes it genesis to Pakistan and began with students of Pashtun origin in Kandahar who were taught in madrassas or religious schools. The situation due to the civil war and lawlessness in the country was ripe for them to make an entry. They had full control of the country by 1996. They imposed their regimented version of Islam and virtually drove women from all work. One of the theories about the local support for the Taliban was that they wanted to bring about some law and order in a country which was beset with internal strife and misgovernance. Hence all their other tenets were overlooked just to ensure that there was rule of law in the country. They were religious bigots too and one of heinous crimes committed by them was the dynamiting of the Bamiyan Buddhas, a cultural heritage that was lost in 2001.

The rule of the Taliban was halted only after the 9/11 terrorist attack on the US, ostensibly plotted by Osama Bin Laden who was being given refuge by the Taliban. The American and their allied forced occupied the country and overthrew the Taliban. However, with their mission accomplished of having eliminated the key conspirators of 9/11 as well as installation of a government, the Americans withdrew in 2021. It was getting too expensive for them to station forces. They did try to train the Afghan forces who would have to fight the Taliban. However, the impending doom could not have been better personified than in the runway at Bagram where some locals desperately clutched onto the wheels of a US plane taking off with the last of the troops. They all fell tragically to their deaths. The Taliban saw the flight of the US troops as an opportunity to reclaim the country. Without the US support, the government in Kabul could not put up a fight against the Taliban and crumbled within a few months. All the training imparted to them seemed futile as the fighters simply rolled in without much opposition into the main cities ending with the fall of Kabul.

The Taliban II phase was supposed to be a milder version of their first avatar. However, this was wishful thinking and they went back to their old conservative ways. They continued to keep women out of most professions as well from the education system, despite the murmurs that they could be different. They continued to impose their harsh version of the Sharia law.

The landlocked country had been an epicentre of a number of invasions from large empires. The land itself was a mixture of provinces, many of who had their own warlords. Moreover, it was also a buffer state in the struggle between the large British and Russian empires.

The behavioral aspect of the people have been moulded by the harsh conditions and the wars that were required to be fought for their survival. This has made the people sturdy and good fighters. The inability of the British empire to conquer this land is a testimony to this courage.

They seemed less interested in expansionism and barring Durrani, no one really went out to conquer other lands. Even the latter returned back to his land after the victory over the Marathas. Why was this so? Maybe empire building was not a primary motive for the people here. Moreover, factionalism was probably a source of worry which prevented them from leaving their kingdom far behind.

As mentioned earlier, the country had been beset with lawlessness and infighting among the various tribes. This could be one of the reasons as to why the Taliban got adequate support in this country. This group focussed a lot on creating a strong legal system, albeit a harsh one which acted as a deterrent to any transgressions. This has been one of the appeals of this group.

To sum up, Afghanistan, has been a classic paradox. Beginning with being the fulcrum of religious and spiritual thought, it transcended to a nation beset with internal strife. These internal differences have been the sole reason why the regimes could not develop it. The Taliban regime on the other hand used this opportunity to restore some semblance of order. Today, it is at a crossroads as the Taliban regime is not recognized primarily due to its harsh laws and treatment of women. Therefore, it provides a lesson that individually being strong and sturdy is not enough if there is no unity and sense of nationhood. The country has also been a centre of the drug trade and this had also had an adverse effect on society.

How has all this history shaped the behavioural pattern of the denizens. The country had been a trading hub for some products and hence there is a keen business sense. The core root of fundamentalism runs as reflected by the Taliban regime for which there is popular support. The general attitude is inward looking and suspicion of the neighbours around. The history of wars and factionalism has been a reason for this. The attitude towards woman and their rights is clearly a big lacuna. Therefore, one cannot reasonably be expected to engage meaningfully on a liberal thought process.

****

CHAPTER TWELVE

The Big Boy syndrome

We would now come to the large nations that straddle the planet. Their thought process on the face of it looks to be structured by the need to maintain their territories or even expand. It needs no rocket science to understand that flexing their muscles is an appropriate strategy for them to flaunt their hegemony.

Moreover, one would expect the regimes to be more dictatorial. The centrality of powers is a sine quo non for maintaining the unity of the provinces. A weak ruler is a recipe for disaster as there is always the threat of regional rebellions.

For one, all these big boys have the inherent genes for being bullies. After all one may question the raison de entre of such powers if they cannot throw their weight around. This is but natural and this creates a frosty relationship with their smaller neighbours. The latter remain skeptical of the intentions and this is the concoction for power struggle.

When power goes to the head, the tendency to poke their nose into others affairs becomes more pronounced. It is about spreading your hegemony or more about thwarting the influence of the other big boys flexing their muscles. The cold war era was one such when both the Soviet Union and the US wanted to exert their sphere of influence and were willing to dirty their hands in regional skirmishes. It unfortunately created some theatres of conflict wherein the smaller players were quashed in this power struggle between the big boys.

Some of these larger nations have believed in expanding and usurping territories. Land grabbing has been their basic prerogative and they continue to do so in the modern era. The concept has been stretched to the sea too as they lay claim to the open oceans. An important part being to control the navigation routes and in a way box out your adversary by controlling their flexibility to traverse the waters.

However, on the other end of the spectrum, these large nations are also susceptible to power struggles. It is not easy to govern a large territory since there are regional aspirations leading to conflict of interest. It creates dissensions and unless ruled with an iron hand, there are tendencies for their weakening. Succession struggles are the most common. It has weakened empires and led to their breakdown. Therefore, the sine quo non becomes the need for good governance and administration.

The behavioural mindset of such large countries varies based on their objectives. A land grabber tends to be aggressive in their dealings with the tendency to look down upon the others with an air of arrogance. They use the interactions as pressure tactics to further their objectives. Some of the these big boys are autocratic in nature which enables them to execute their plans with little opposition.

But on the other end of the spectrum, you do have other large nations who do not harbour such expansionist ambitions. Those with democratic institutions have checks and balances within the system that stops them for going out on misadventures.

The historical evolution of these countries is a barometer of how they think. On one end of the spectrum are the power hungry land grabbers who display the sense of arrogance and look down upon the others. There are others who are powerful and use this clout to spread their political thoughts or thwart the dissemination of the school of the opposite thought. Then there are the others who show more magnamity but this has the danger of the neighbours taking them for granted.

Therefore, this spectrum also manifests in different behavioural patterns. It ranges from arrogance to bullying tactics to being receptive and amicable with others across the borders.

****

• 55 •

****

CHAPTER THIRTEEN

Zhongguo

Unlike most of the other kingdoms in the eastern hemisphere, the Chinese dynasties premised their geo-political thought on land grabbing. They had mastered the art of expansionism and this has filtered down to the present communist regime. It would be appropriate to look at the history of the country in order to gauge its geo-political strategy. Even Napoleon was aware of this and one of his famous quotes about the country is *"China is a sleeping giant. Let her sleep, for when she wakes she will move the world."* The country has now literally moved the world by expanding its geographical spread.

Chinese thought process on expansionism could be traced to the mandarin name of the country itself. China is known as **Zhongguo**, whereby Zhong translates into *"the centre of the world"* and Guo is *"country"*. Thus Chong Quo (or Zhongguo) would literally mean that it is a country at the centre of the world or is the Middle Kingdom. This may well be interpreted as the centrality of China in global affairs. This has been stretched by its policy makers of late to subtly look at domination over the other cultures. This is an indirect reference to both the geo-centricity of the country and the fact that global growth has to take place around it.

A related aspect to this is the concept of Han chauvinism, including that of the *"Great Han"*. It is also believed that the Han people are at the centre of mankind. This has been the basis on which the concept of expansionism including through the settlement of the Han people in the annexed territories has been propagated.

Chinese expansion in the communist regime has also been inspired by the concept of Lebensraum which was the bedrock for the Nazi expansion too. Chinese civilisations have always propagated this idea and engaged in wars with neighbours to assert their influence and dominance. The frontiers of the Kingdom have always been the subject of intense interest both with a view to send a chilling message to any misadventure that might be attempted as also the need to expand.

The Qin dynasty in 221BC, laid the edifice of this principle as it united the Han kingdoms into the region. It also made contact with the ancient Yue tribes and original denizens of the Korean peninsula. Subsequently, the Han dynasty, which ruled from 206BC to 220AD conquered North Korea and North Vietnam while also making foray into some parts of modern Xinjiang. The period of these dynasties also saw the tremendous economic and cultural progress such as the building of the Great Wall, emergence of writing, standardization of weights and measures, creation of a centralized bureaucracy, development of agriculture, creation of the Silk Route for trade with the Roman Empire, papermaking, astronomy and metallurgy.

After a hiatus due to the population loss and the need for consolidation, the Sui dynasty, which came in 581AD then attempted to conquer Korea but its campaign was cut short. They also created infrastructure facilities such as the Grand Canal and making and repair of sections of the Great Wall to prevent invasion from the North. The Tang dynasty, which rules from 618-907AD, went into its expansionist mode recapturing Korea and North Vietnam while making forays into Xinjiang and Tibet. However, it vacated the latter. With the collapse of the Tang dynasty, most of its acquisitions including Vietnam became independent. In the 13th century, the Yuan dynasty then went into an expansionist spree even invading the Pagan kingdom in modern Myanmar. It had successes in Korea and Tibet.

However, it was in the 17th century when the Qing dynasty established the largest sphere of influence of the Chinese kingdoms. The Qings were ironically Manchus from the Manchuria region who united through large grouping called banners. However, they also assimilated the Han Chinese into their administrative structures. They conquered the frontiers, piggybacking on the strong cavalry and artillery. This neutralised the advantages of the nomadic horsemen, such as those of the Dzunghar Khanate in the Central Asian Steppes. One of the largest historical genocides, estimated to be over a million, that of the Dzunghars, was undertaken during this period by this dynasty.

The Qings made successful forays into Mongolia, Tibet and Xinjiang. They attacked Korea and some of the regions in modern Kazakhstan, Kyrgyzstan and Tajikistan. They even managed to invade Taiwan and capture the island. The territorial expansion went to the extent of them even claiming the island of Sakhalin.

The Qings however had to taste defeat in Myanmar during 1765-1769. However, despite this, they harboured ambitions of making it part of their territory. After the collapse of the Qing dynasty in 1911, the Republic of China took over the reins. However, both outer Mongolia and Tibet declared their independence but were not recognised by the former.

It was a period of consolidation but external influences such as that of the Japanese empire was felt. The collapse of the Qings also led to the vacuum in power that was exploited by both Japan and the Soviet Union. The Japanese tried to control some key parts of China through the 21 point demand made during 1915 at the time of World War 1. They also attacked Manchuria in 1931 in a guise of a staged incident. The Soviets fought a battle for control of the China Eastern Railway which led to them defeating the army of the Republic in 1929.

However, World War II changed the dynamics with the Republic trying to assert its influence in Korea and South East Asia. A foray was also made into North Vietnam but the Chinese civil war saw the overthrow of the Republic and takeover by the communist

People's Republic. This was the turning point for expansionism as the Communists poked their nose and engaged to expand across all territories. They also smartly used the window of opportunity in this period when all the colonial powers were licking their wounds after the devastating economic effect of World War II.

The conquest of Xinjiang was undertaken with ease including with the support from the Soviets. This was because the latter wanted peace with the Central Asian countries and did not make any attempts to halt the Chinese expansion. The only resistance came from the Turkistan Republic but that was overcome and the death of their crème-de-la-crème in a plane crash facilitated the takeover. Communist China immediately occupied Xinjiang in 1949 and the Turkistan Republic movement also petered out. The People's Republic of China (PRC) then pursued a policy of settlement of the Han and Hui Chinese in the Dzungharia region thereby altering the demographic profile. The tensions with the Ugyhur's also rose and there were allegations of cultural cleansing of the latter.

Forays were made into Tibet as the Communist forces nibbled territories along the border with Tibet. They attacked the Chomdo region in October, 1950 and forced some Tibetan representatives in Beijing to sign a 17 point agreement that established their suzerainty over Tibet. Moreover, they also captured the Amdo and Kham region integrating them into their provinces and stationed a large number of troops in central Tibet. The US made a weak attempt in 1956-57 to support the Tibetan resistance but it petered out since the airdropped leaders were captured. Even the Russians supported the Chinese in the bombing of Lhasa and other towns. Eventually in 1959 when the palace was surrounded, the Dalai Lama was forced to flee to India and the territory was annexed.

North Vietnam was another theatre where the People's Republic ventured by supporting North Vietnam. This war lasted two decades with the victory of the North Vietnamese forces in 1975. The Chinese could thus not implement their expansionism here since there were too many players in the fray after the defeat of the US. Nevertheless, the installation of a communist government in the country was the next best option to which the Chinese had to reconcile with.

The Korean war was however, an opportunity for them to showcase their military prowess. With the colonial powers decimated by the war, US was the only real powerhouse at that time and even they were given a tough fight. While the latter managed to save South Korea, they were pushed back from the North Korean territory by the Chinese who even managed to take Seoul a few times. The battle of the Chosin Reservoir, made famous by a movie, showed their prowess in multi-pronged and flanking attacks on even the mighty US ground forces. While they suffered heavy casualties in that, they were able to chase off the strong Americans from North Korea. This would surely have given them lots of confidence to complete the other territorial conquests such as Tibet.

Communist China subsequently waged a war against India in 1962 and captured the region of Aksai Chin in Ladakh. Without the knowledge of the Indians who lacked intelligence, they even made a highway in the disputed territory without even a war. They also took over Arunachal Pradesh which they argued was part of South Tibet but retreated. China again asserted in 1967 its claim over Sikkim which was then an Indian protectorate. There were two skirmishes at Nathu La and Cho La during September-October, 1967. While the versions are different, as in any such incident, India managed to hold onto its position and the Sikkim-Tibet border got effectively resolved after this. Sikkim eventually integrated into India in 1975.

Subsequently in 1974, China also engaged in a battle for the Paracel Islands with Vietnam. They managed to inflict heavy damage on the South Vietnamese navy and capture these islands. It was possibly the first full scale sea battle that the Chinese were engaged in and for the first time showed the prowess of their naval forces. The salami slicing technique used in the Spratly Islands in a multi country dispute exposed their classic re-adaptation of the

Lebensraum by brute show of force.

China has been historically applying the principle of Lebensraum in its own subtle way trying to chip away and usurp territory of kingdoms around it. While not openly propagating it, the strategy has been to wage battles, use the classic colonial principle of divide and rule and change the demographics of the region by settlement of Chinese from elsewhere. The latter has been supplemented with the security mechanism provided to these settlers.

Another smart tactic used by them has been to use any world crisis as an appropriate entry point. The rest of the world would then be embroiled in the crisis and they could subtly achieved their territorial ambitions without any resistance. Some of the classic cases are that of Tibet when the 1950s says little appetite from the World War adversaries to engage meaningfully. Moreover, US was also embroiled in the Korean war which was an opportune time to enter in 1950. The two front war with India is another classic example when the Chinese used the Cuban missile crisis for an opportune time to enter and attack India. Even in the 2022 Ukraine crisis when the Russians have been trying to capture the former, they have been toying around with the idea of annexation of Taiwan as both the US and its NATO allies seek to defuse the crisis. It is only on account of the active patrolling by the US warships in the Taiwan straits that the ambition is still on hold.

They have understood that security is one of the primary tools to ensure the success of this nibbling away strategy. Hence, even today wherever China seeks to make investment, especially in areas prone to law and order problems, they have taken their security apparatus with them and establish their own little self-contained fiefdoms.

Being the shrewd businessmen that they are, they have also put in place systems for ensuring an increased debt burden and then set in place a recovery mechanism. This classic tactic takes us back to our colonial days when the powers that be used the same mechanism to bleed the economy and usurp assets like land.

On the social front, the Chinese have used the tactics of intimidation to suppress the local resistance movements. This has been through dividing the resistance movements as well as perpetuating atrocities on the vulnerable sections like women. Taking a cue from the Qing dynasty's maltreatment of Ughyur women including raping them, the Chinese have continued to use the strategy in both Tibet and Xinjiang.

Moreover, they have, like the colonial powers created infrastructure in these regions primarily with a view to ensure easy access for their military forces, in case of any emergency situation. It has also facilitated settlements by attracting the Han Chinese to these regions. However, it is important to also give credit to the Chinese for having changed the entire connectivity of the regions they conquered, even in treacherous conditions and altitudes like Tibet. This has definitely given a fillip to the economy of these regions and improved their growth parameters, even if the same has not been equitous for the original denizens of those lands.

The Chinese have also used historical references of their dynasties to justify their expansion. Chiefly, it has been the Yuan and Qing dynasties whose rule over these disputed regions which has been used as a rationale for China to usurp territories. What is significant to note that the Qing dynasty which has been the bedrock of the Chinese historian's justification for annexing Tibet and Xinjiang was founded by the Manchu bannermen who originate from the Manchuria region of Mongolia.

However, at the end of it all, one must give credit to the country for becoming an economic powerhouse and changing the global balance of power especially after the threat of a unilateral centric power with the breakup of the Soviet Union. Moreover, with the Russia-Ukraine war, the Chinese seized an opportunity to create their own bloc to act as a counterweight to the west. They have aligned closer to the Russians, played a key role in the expansion of the BRICS, made huge investments in the Belt and Road Initiative (BRI), made forays into African nations though the means of aid and technology etc. They continue to threaten Taiwan and have made clear their ambition to occupy it. One of the key drivers for taking Taiwan is that it is the hub of the semi-conductor industry with prowess in fab manufacturing. The industry is key to technological development and the Chinese still do not have the complete value chain. Many thus view the annexation of Taiwan as a geo-politico-techno strategy of the communist party.

China's growth and impressive development has also been fuelled by the little resistance and the dictatorial way in which opposing voices are suppressed. Take over of land has never been a problem in the country since no one dare raise a voice against the communist party. Even many of the celebrities who voiced some opposition like the businessmen Jack Ma, actress Zhao Wei and tennis player Peng Shuai faced the ire of the administration and literally disappeared from the scene. Unlike in democracies, no project gets stalled in the absence of any dissent. The Communist Party is all powerful and nearly every Chinese aspires to become a Member after their schooling. The membership is a passport to a career growth for everyone including the bureaucrats.

While traversing the country, one can feel that there is an air of suspicion or mistrust. It would seem that people are guarded in what they say. It would be surprise for people coming from vibrant democracies who are used to airing their views with greater freedom. There is a high possibility of conversations being tapped, whether in hotels or in public transport. This has been vindicated by one of the incidents faced by developing country negotiators in a tier 2 city of China when they were going to a mall from their hotel in a taxi. When they reached the destination, the taxi driver pressed the wrong button and their entire recorded conversation during the trip was being replayed. They got the shock of their lives and kept mum till they returned to their country. On enquiry from others, it was found out that this was not uncommon and the taxi drivers were instructed and probably paid for recording conversation of foreigners.

Thus coming to the behavioural pattern, one of the aspects is that they are shrewd as far as business deals are concerned.

However, given the background of the communist rule, there is a strange air of distrust as one moves around the country. Despite the rapid economic growth, the denizens are cautious of foreigners and tend to show off the prosperity of the nation. The independent thought process is clearly lacking and are in a way brainwashed by their leaders. Even the Dalai Lama, who probably has not even picked up a gun, is considered a terrorist by most citizens based on what is fed to them. Finally, the concept of land grabbing is ingrained in the psyche and this would be reflected in any geopolitical discussions with them. Overall, it is a strange concoction of being in an economically developed region where one needs to exercise caution and leave back home the hat of critical thinking.

CHAPTER FOURTEEN

The Land Down Under

Australia is actually the 7th largest nation in the world as well as continent. Far south, it is closer to Antarctica than the mainland of Asia. The low population density and the rich wealth of mineral resources makes it an ideal location that is likely to be one of the future epicentres of growth in the world. However, for those wishing to leverage this, it is important to gauge the behavioural pattern of its denizens.

The human history of this vast expanse started some 65,000 years back when the Aboriginals settled here and even went to the southern island of Tasmania. The were probably the first mariners in human history. Archeological remains point to the use of tools like axes, fibre, net as well as the presence of rock art and religious rituals. The climatic and landform changes forced a lot of migration and cultural changes among the Aborginals. Due to the temperature variations and rise in sea levels, many islands such as Tasmania and the Torres were formed and many communities got separated. This is believed to have occurred around 14,000 years back. It also made them develop the unique cultures which were premised on territorial boundaries and clan identity. Subsequently, those who inhabited the northern part of the continent and known as the Torres Strait Islanders are believed to have come around 4000 years back from Papua New Guinea with settlements coming around 2500 years back.

The European immigration occurred in 1606 through Willem Janzsoon, the Dutch navigator who came to its northern shores. The

Dutch explorers further went to the southern and western shores and named it as New Holland. The name of the land however came from the Portuguese explorer Querois in honour of the Queen of Austria though he had landed in Vanuatu and thought it to be the fabled southern land. It was however, the Dutch explorers who mapped much of this vast land from the western part to the northern and southern regions including Tasmania, New Zealand and Fiji.

The British influence began with William Dampier in 1688 and James Cook who came in 1770 to the eastern coast and claimed it for his country. The next wave of British flotilla based on Cook's information came to Botany Bay and in 1788 settled prisoners from British jails in what is known as a penal colony. The French also made their foray into the continent, first with Tasmania by the explorer Fresne. Subsequently, Louis Alouarn lay claim to Western Australia but it was not colonized.

The establishment of a penal colony was a well thought out decision by the British. The proposal first came from John Callendar in 1766 who argued that one could exploit the riches of the land. With the American Civil War, there was loss of land and hence an alternative was being explored to settle convicts. One of these was the African colonies ranging from Gambia to Namibia. The economic argument of the Southern continent being suitable for sugar, cotton and tobacco plantations as well as sourcing of hemp, flax and timber from New Zealand was put forth. A decision was finally taken in 1786 with many theories being floated ranging from seeking an alternative, economic rationale due to the trade potential, agricultural produce, strategic location etc. The last point was mooted due to the alliance of the other naval powers like the Dutch, French and Spanish which necessitated a British naval base in the region.

After this the penal colony came up which slowly expanded around the period 1820-1850. This was both the expansion of the British rule which covered nearly all the existing provinces except Western Australia as well as the settlers moving beyond the boundaries of their colonies. These settlements became self-sustaining too. The expansions went into Tasmania in order to counter the French influence. Victoria with the region of Melbourne became a hot spot for settlement due to the rich grasslands. Western Australia was a centre of Dutch and French rule before Major Lockyer annexed it in 1827 for the British crown. South Australia was established as a British colonial province in 1836 but was taken over by the crown in 1844 as it went through an economic turmoil and clash with the indigenous communities. Queensland emerged as a separate province in 1859 due to disputes by the settlers with the government in Sydney and the aborigines.

The Europeans then went deep into the continent and their interaction with the Aboriginals was a disaster for the latter due to both disease and conflict. The smallpox outbreaks along with measles, typhoid, influenza and tuberculosis took a big toll on the indigenous population due to their low level of immunity. The Britishers were the ones who expanded their influence and managed to establish six colonies. This was also fuelled by the gold rush and the growth of agriculture based industries.

The provinces had their own political set up but circumstances were developing for their eventual unification. This was driven by the natives association of largely British settlers who wanted to unite the provinces. These natives over time were largely of British and Irish heritage. They were nationalists who wanted the British identity to continue and only a minority wanted a separate identity. It was these nationalists who sowed the concept of "*White Australia*". A form of racism which sought to keep out all outsiders and promote the concept of the country being for the whites, almost all from British descent. This also stemmed from the need to keep out the French and German ambitions which led to a unified defence force and a railway line. There were however some stark differences in the provinces ranging from free trade proponents to protectionist ones. There was also an element of suspicion on the possible domination of New South Wales and Victoria is such an alliance.

These British colonies voted in 1901 to establish a federation and the country came into being. It was part of the Commonwealth and fought in the World Wars. Some of the measures introduced after it became a federation were conservative and sometimes racist ones like keeping out of Asian immigration, repatriation of indentured sugar labour from Queensland, exclusion of Aboriginal suffrage if they had not voted in the state jurisdiction, tariffs on goods etc. The population increase due to migration during the early years of the federation was on account of the white British population which was allowed to settle there. The migration policy also saw a lot of Europeans, from the south and eastern part settling in the country. Even this was not a smooth transition with the bestseller *"They are a Weird Mob"* by John O Grady, having a satirical reflection of how the immigrants must assimilate into the Australian culture.

The *"White Australian policy"* thus remained manifested in many forms. Even the first prime minister Edmund Barton justified it by quoting, *"The doctrine of the equality of man was never intended to apply to the equality of the Englishman and the Chinaman."*

Australia participated in both the World Wars with great gusto. In the first war, they engaged against the German armies and the Ottoman Empire. They fought along with New Zealand under the umbrella of the ANZAC forces. In the second World War, the fighting was both in the European and Pacific fronts. They even faced bombings by the Japanese but managed to hold out.

The policy of cultural assimilation of 1951 further eroded the rights of the aborigines. The subsequent period also saw the removal of children of the mixed descent people. This was justified on the basis of welfare measures. It is estimated that nearly 1/10th of the entire indigenous population was left scarred by this measure. This left the society of the indigenous people shattered. It ruptured their very cultural ethos.

In the cold war era, the country allied with the United States. It continued its strong relationship with its erstwhile colonial master. Its forces played a key role in the Korean war, Vietnamese civil war,

Malayan emergency, Suez crisis etc. A trilateral security treaty with the US in 1951 was to act as a counterweight to Japanese influence and laid the foundation of the foreign policy of the country. With UK, it was a tacit show of support but the formers 1973 accession to the European market was a blow to many conservative Australians. They had always seen the other Europeans as potential threats given the history of the struggle with the British over their lands.

The *"White Australian Policy"* however, remained and was reformed only during the 1972 labour government. The new policy looked at closer ties with the Asia Pacific region with proximal countries like Indonesia. It also recognized Communist China which laid the foundation for the relationship between the two countries. For the indigenous people, there was a policy of self-determination in social, economic and political issues. The quantum of funding was increased by more than five times on Aboriginal services. Finally, a Commission was set up on the land rights in the Northern Territory. Subsequently, an Act on the land rights was passed in 1976.

This was the fruition of the struggle of the indigenous people. However, their economic integration remains far from over. The plight of the Aborigines in the big cities of the country is a testimony to this. Without providing them sustainable economic opportunities to be self-dependent, they are given out weekly doles which get over. Then they resort to begging and even other forms of illegal activities in the big cities. Neville Bonner, the first indigenous MP had said, *"The White Australia Policy was a clear message that Indigenous Australians were not considered part of the nation's future. Its abolition was a necessary step towards reconciliation."*

Moreover, the White Australia Policy may have gone away on paper but remains ingrained in the mindset even today. There is a level of racism in the society and non-whites do not have the same level of receptivity as the others. In some cases, it is overtly evident and the people who stay there would testify. Honest feedback from service workers like those who drive vehicles, work in the commercial establishment or utility sector would reveal this.

The mindset cannot be better captured than that of the White Australian Policy. There is an attitude of suspicion and deprecation to those who have a different racial tone. It is about the need to make them assimilate into the Aussie culture. Moreover, the aggression levels are also on an average higher, probably fuelled by the pub culture. Hopefully, nothing to do with the history of being a penal colony. The treatment of the indigenous people is however the biggest source of worry. While on paper, it looks hunky dory but the ground situation is very different. There is always of cultural clash with the rest of the population. Giving out doles seem to the pillar on which the policy is justified. But there is no economic freedom or opportunity provided. There are no schemes for skilling of these people for jobs which they could do well in.

What can one do in such circumstances? Be prepared for undercurrents of weird behaviour if you are a non-white. Unexpected phases of aggressive behaviour can be manifested. As for the indigenous population, the racial undertones are more prominent. In the Aussie mind, they are treated quite differently, obviously with a lot of deprecation. They have not been integrated into the mainstream of society and have been worse off than the Maoris across the straits.

****

CHAPTER FIFTEEN

Canada

A country known for its sparse population, sub-zero conditions, array of lakes and expansive forests. Flanked by the United States to the south and the Artic polar cap on the north, it is one of the largest nations of the world. The tough climatic conditions has also seen a wave of immigration without any filters since they needed human resources to work on the land.

It is on the last continent of human habitation. The earliest humans are supposed to have migrated from Siberia over the Bering land bridge during a glaciation period and falling sea levels around 50,000 years ago. An ice sheet kept them in the Alaska and Yukon region. It was only during the melting of this ice sheet around 16,000 years ago that further ingress into the south, in what is modern Canada was made.

With the stabilization of the climatic conditions, there were many historic civilisations that came up. It began with the Woodland cultural period around 2000 BC, which was known for its pottery. The Hopewell tradition then came around the river banks and the shores of Lake Ontario. The Algonquian and Iroquian people then settled in the eastern part of the country. They were supposed to have come from the US States of Idaho and Montana.

The central plains saw the habitation of the Cree people who were primarily bison hunters. The northwest was populated by those speaking the Na-Dene language, which is supposed to have its roots from the Yenisey region of Russia. British Colombia saw people who spoke the Salishan language. This region has abundant fish and there was the tradition of whaling. The Dorset people inhabited the Arctic north around 500 BC with the Inuits stated to be their ancestors.

The first wave of Europeans that came to the region were the Norse, who came from Greenland and Iceland around 1000AD. They made the settlements around Newfoundland.

John Cabot was the British explorer who landed in the country in June, 1497 on the basis of a letter from the King. He is said to have landed in Cape Bonivista in Newfoundland. His son Sebastian continued these trysts for the British Empire. In 1583, Humprey Gilbert claimed St Johns, Newfoundland by a royal prerogative. Cupids, Ferryland and Virginia were established as settlements subsequently. In 1621, rights were granted to get settlers from Scotland in a new colony. However, these settlements known as Nova Scotia fructified in 1629. In the struggle with the French, it was finally ceded to the latter. In 1670, the Hudson's Bay company lay claim to the area around the Hudson bay known as Ruperts land. However, in the ensuring battles with the French, the Britishers were able to recapture Nova Scotia and Rupert Land in 1710. On the western side, James Cook had already chartered the coast upto Alaska. The region saw a boom in trade of sea otter pelts to China. Spain also laid claim to this region but by 1789, this was settled in favour of the British empire. The chartering of the territories of Vancouver island in 1849, Queen Charlotte Islands in 1853 and British Colombia in 1858 occurred.

Spain also claimed rights to the lands visited by Cabot by the Treaty of Tordesillas with Portugal. Despite this treaty, the latter still visited many lands in Newfoundland and Nova Scotia in an aim to establish rights over these. However, with the passage of time, the Portuguese concentrated on the unexplored lands in South America, chiefly Brazil.

The French landed in 1524 with Verrazano's expedition sponsored by King Francis I. In 1534 Jaques Cartier then claimed lands for France. He also sailed along the St Lawrence waterway to reach the present day Montreal. However, the attempts for claiming proved futile. In 1604, the fur trade sparked another series of adventures by Pierre da Gua as his team led by Samuel Champlain mapped the US east coast. In these efforts, the cities of Saint John, New Brunswick, St John River and Quebec city came up. He made tremendous discoveries and was also involved in a conflict with the Iruquois after siding with the Hurons. In the next phase, the Sulpicans in 1642 established the town of Ville Marie, the present day Montreal. It was in 1663 that the French royalty took hold of these colonies. However, post this period while the population of settlers grew significantly, there was little immigration from France. Most of these settlements happened along the St-Lawrence river. The settlements from England and Scotland on the other hand ensured that the French settlement was only around 10% of the total population. In 1686, Perre Troyes challenged the Hudson Bay company and managed to capture some outposts. France also lay claim to the Mississippi river valley by establishing some outposts in terms of forts.

In the ensuing battle between the British and the French from 1688 to 1743, the latter lost a lot of territories. Nova Scotia as well as Rupert land was lost in 1710. The French made their reinforcements in Louisbourg to protect the entry into the St Lawrence river. However, in 1745, William Peppernell led an army and defeated the French here. However, they retained the fort due to a peace treaty. The Britishers also fought a war against the Acadians who were French settlers in Nova Scotia and managed to expel them. Nova Scotia eventually got demographically transitioned with closer ties to New England. The French were defeated in 1759 in Quebec and the city of Montreal fell in 1760. In the final nail in the coffin for the French Empire, the Treaty of Paris signed in 1763 literally removed any land rights. They only had fishing rights in New Foundland as well as the islands of Saint Pierre and Miquelon. In an irony, the French considered the sugar producing Guadeloupe as more important than the vast country which they traded off in the Treaty. Voltaire's famous phrase for Canada *"quelques arpents de neige"* translated as "a *few acres of snow*" summed up the importance that the French attached to this land. However, to the credit of the Britishers, they preserved the French Civil Law through the Quebec Act 1774.

The American Revolution had a profound effect on Canadian history. The invasion of Quebec by the rebels was repulsed in 1775. However, by 1781, it was clear that Britain would have to give up its American colonies. Thus many of the loyalists were settled in New Brunswick in 1784. Quebec was also divided between the French speaking south and the Anglophonic north in 1791. The period also saw a wave of American farmers who were searching for new lands settling here. The 1783 Treaty saw the demarcation of the Canada-US boundary; ceding of many states in the province of Quebec such as Michigan, Wisconsin, Illinois, Indiana and Ohio to the US; and grant of fishing rights along the coast of Newfoundland and Grand Banks. Then came the 1812 war between the Americans and the British that was also concentrated on the Canadian border since the aim was to drive off the imperial power from the continent. While the boundaries were preserved, there was reverse migration and threats to the existing immigrants due to the republican values. It was from this phase onwards that the country harboured suspicion towards the intentions of their southern neighbour who wanted to drive out the British.

Then came the phase of the struggle against the colonial rulers in both Upper and Lower Canada beginning in 1837 with reformers like Mackenzie. Nearly all the major provinces and towns like Quebec City, Montreal. The outcome of all this was the creation of the United Province of Canada by 1840 and the establishment of a responsible government by 1848. A wave of migrations happened from the British Isles chiefly England, Ireland and Scotland.

The pathway to the establishment of Canada came about in 1864 with the Quebec and Charlotteville conferences as the British colonies were united into a federation. The formal process came about through the British North America Act of 1867. The drivers of this move were the need for a formidable defence, access across the vast countryside through railroad connections, loyalist culture including for the French speaking parts, fear of expansion of the US and the desire for a responsible government. The process of incorporation of the provinces was slow since all did not benefit from the Pacific railroad. There was also a sense of suspicion between the Anglophone and Francophone denizens. Some of the last provinces to join in were Alberta and Saskatchewan, primarily on account of they being the bread basket with settlements from people of Ukrainian as well as other European countries. The 1931 Statute of Westminster acknowledged Canada at being on par with United Kingdom and laid the foundation stone for its recognition. Eventually, the 1982 Canada Act provided the full sovereignty of the country.

The relationship with the indigenous people also known as the First Nation was the most complex political situation that the government had to tackle. The Treaties signed actually removed the land rights of these people and confined them to specific reserves. It opened up the rest of the areas for settlement, something akin to their southern neighbour.

World War 1 was an acid test for the federation as helping the British did not have the support of the Francophones of Quebec. Hence conscription became a challenge. It eventually pressed for a place in the peace conference after the war. This was reluctantly handed over despite initial reservations of both the Americans and British. It was also a reflection of the country looking at playing a larger global role. In World War 2 too, Canada was heavily involved as it sent it forces to fight both the Germans and the Japanese. There was a crisis of conscription between the English and French speakers in this war too. However, a more significant aspect was the fact that it got close to the US on account of the development of the Alaskan highway and the air bases on New Foundland.

Canadian behaviour stems from a lot of factors namely the admixture of British and French culture, language factor, harsh weather, relationship with their southern neighbour and the need to get in immigrants to work in these adverse conditions. The first factor is an example of how they have a deadly combination of

British arrogance and stiff upper lip with the shrewdness and sweet talk of the French. The relationship with the immigrants has been a hot and cold one. They are needed given the low population density and the harsh conditions but deep within, the racist behaviour resides. They are an important vote bank too and the Canadians have no qualms in encouraging those with extremist and secessionist views too. All with a motive of pin pricking developing countries like India. The relationship with the US has been a difficult one. While they got close during World War II, there persists that level of mistrust given the latter's global political clout. Culturally, it is rich with both the British and French influence.

****

CHAPTER SIXTEEN

Russia

A superpower, which is now in a difficult phase of its history, had an interesting storyline. The largest country despite the disintegration of the Soviet Union, there is no doubt that it has lost some of its sheen. This despite the fact that it has abundant natural resources and arguably the most scientifically oriented human resources.

It all began with the Rus state being established in 862AD by the Eastern Slavs. Kiev was the de-facto capital during 882 AD under the rule of Prince Oleg. Christianity percolated from the Byzantine empire at the end of the first millenium and the fusion with Slavic culture is what led to the unique Orthodox form of the religion.

The Mongol Invasion of 1237AD led to the collapse of the Rus but post that, one saw the emergence of Moscow as a political and cultural centre. The process of unification also began around this time. By the end of the 15th century, the Grand Duchy of Moscow had united most of the region under the reign of Ivan the Great.

The Tsars then emerged with Ivan the Terrible in 1547 but succession battles after him left the region in a chaos. It was the Romanov dynasty in 1613 which brought a semblance of order. It was during this dynastic rule that the conquests of Siberia and far east right upto the Pacific coast began. However, a lot of resistance was met with regional satraps such as the Cossacks. The name of the country came about in 1721 during the reign of Peter the Great with St Petersburg being the capital. There was an infusion of European culture during this period. This could actually be termed as the Russian Renaissance era. An invasion by Napolean, who had actually occupied Moscow for a brief period, was repulsed and this added to the aura of the Russian empire.

The subsequent period leading upto the Russian revolution of 1917 was a period of turmoil starting with the peasant revolution. Despite attempts at economic and political reforms, the Tsars wanted to hold onto their powers and refused to devolve it. This set the stage for the revolution as Lenin took over the reigns of the country. It also saw the formation of the Soviet Union which was an amalgamation of Russia, Ukraine, Byelorussia and the Trans Caucasian regions. The country became a communist regime and this lay the start of its divorce from capitalist Europe. The political relations began souring and this was the start of a different version of the modern cold war. The country however grew economically and this was a period of stability.

Even before the start of World War II, the political relations with western Europe or the US was strained as there was suspicion about the communist regime and its influence.

However, ironically, it was the Nazi regime that forced both these allies to come together to take on a greater danger. It was under Stalin, a man loathed as an autocrat in of world history who was at the helm of the reins during this most trying times. While western historians may scoff, the greatest phase of Russian history was the resistance to the Nazi blitzkrieg during World War II. After being overrun by the German forces, the resistance began around the cities of Leningrad, Moscow and Stalingrad. The defeats of the Germans there was what turned the tide of the entire war. The Soviet Red Army and its civilians suffered the maximum casualties during this war, around 27 million, and bore the brunt of the ground and air attacks. One striking difference here was that Soviet women were in the forefront of the war including snipping and use of arms. It was this defeat that broke the morale of the Germans who were on an ascendancy in the war and they capitulated. The Red Army counterattacked and ensured the fall of Berlin. The war on the Eastern front brought out the grit and determination of the people. It showed the unity of the country and how it could take losses and still hang on. Many right wing historians have tried to paint a picture of the Soviets not caring for their dead and undertaking atrocities on the captured German civilians especially women in the counterattack. It is all a matter of perception but there is no doubt that but for the Soviets, the World War II may have taken a different course in history.

The post war phase rather than uniting the victors led to a cold war era where both the Soviets and the Americans went through an arms race equipping themselves with nuclear weapons. The Eastern European countries were under the influence of the former in what was known as the Warsaw block. Politically, the Soviets continued with their communist ideology and were left behind in the economic growth story that the capitalist west witnessed. Nevertheless, they were very powerful with the weaponry they had. This phase also saw both the Soviets and the Americans interfere in many regional conflicts ranging from Korea to Cuba to Afghanistan. Some of these proved costly for the Soviets draining their resources. The Bay of Pigs incident in Cuba brought them very close to confrontation with the Americans but it got resolved. The retreat from Afghanistan was necessitated by the huge costs being incurred as the Mujahideen were well funded by the west through Pakistan.

The economy also went through a difficult phase and the political structure was also weak. This necessitated perestroika or reforms under Gorbachev wherein the Soviets disintegrated as the communist party became weak. Russia became an independent country and so did all the others including the Central Asian Republics. However, this did have the pernicious effect of making the world unipolar as the US led west became powerful. It was only in the early part of the 21st century when China became a powerful entity both economically and militarily that the balance was restored. With the Ukraine war, Russia had greater challenges on its plate. However, geo-political realignments are once again happening with the Russians being part of the power centre around China. The latter have played their cards smartly as they are looking at other allies too like Iran, Turkey and countries in Sub-Saharan

Africa. They are all part of the neo cold war.

With the weakening of the Russian geo political hold after the breakup of the Soviet Union, they resorted to a new form of military diplomacy. The state funded some private militias to influence Russian policy globally. The Wagner Group headed by the late Yevgeny Prigozhin was the instrument used to be part of the civil wars in Central African Republic, Libya, Mali, Syria and Ukraine. In the Ukraine conflict, they played a key role. However, it was this war that saw their downfall as the Group attempted to mutiny in response to their dissatisfaction with the Russian strategy. Prigozhin and the top Wagner brass died in a plane crash but it is suspected that he was assassinated. However, the use of this private militia has been one of the strategies used by Russia to exert its geopolitical influence.

Behaviourally, the Russian revolution and the communist regime has had a profound effect on society. There is an element of skepticism through which the Russians view others, albeit not to the same extent as probably a China or North Korea. This element would always be part of the behavioral trait. Moreover, the country has a powerful set of oligarchs who have been kept under reins by the regime in order to counter any political aspirations they harbour. However, with their wealth, they do influence the economy of the country. Therefore, while dealing on economic matters including trade diplomacy, one has keep in mind the power of these oligarchs. In terms of other behavioural patterns, the Russians are warm and hospitable. They are not typically the businessmen and would like to build up relations over the long term. They remain fiercely patriotic and are proud of their role in defeating Nazi Germany in World War II.

****

CHAPTER SEVENTEEN

Yankees

Arguably the most liberal country of the globe, the history of the United States has reflected this transition from a colony to being the most powerful nation. Despite all the criticism, it remains the most attractive nation for immigration. Moreover, there is a filtering as far as quality is concerned as its higher institutions of learning are a magnet for the crème-de la crème of the globe.

The nation saw the first settlement of people around 15,000 years back possibly from Russia through the Bering sea. They trudged all the way through Alaksa, Yukon and then Canada before making their way to the country. The indigenous people slowly settled in these lands starting off as hunters and slowly getting into agriculture plantations. The period also saw a number of tribes inhabiting the breadth and width of the country.

The Mississippians were a famous tribe around the 12th century which had a population of 20,000 and saw a significant social stratification. Communities came up in the Pacific Northwest while the Iroquois came up around New York. The latter were powerful and conquered many of the other tribes. Hawaii was probably discovered by the Tahitian explorers in the 13th century with the Britishers arriving there in 1778.

There is a belief that the Norse explorer Leif Erikson came to Vinland or the East Coast around 1000AD. Christopher Colombus came to the continent in 1492. Subsequently, the Spanish explored inland including the Grand Canyon and even founded the modern city of Los Angeles in the west coast. The first of the British settlements came around in 1607. The Dutch East India company also got a foothold here by establishing New Amsterdam in the Manhattan island that was purchased from the indigenous people. However, they came in conflict with the British who took over New York in 1664. The Swedish also came here and established colonies although they were overrun by the Dutch. While the French were largely confined to Canada, they too settled in parts of Louisiana.

The British foray were a mix of settlers ranging from private business groups to those escaping political and religious persecutions and finally convicts. Jamestown in Virginia was the first settlement in 1607. After a series of attacks by the indigenous Powhatan, the settlements came under the royal umbrella. The Puritans escaping religious persecution settled in New England. Settlements also sprung up in Massachusetts Bay, Rhode Island, Connecticut River Valley, New Hampshire and Maine. The Middle colonies of New York, New Jersey and Delaware came up in the 1660s. The religious dissenters like Quakers, Methodists and Amish settled in Pennsylvania. Towards the south, Maryland came up in 1632, Carolina in 1670 and Georgia in 1712.

By the middle of the 18th century, there were 13 British colonies along the east coast and some along the southern coast. They was a governor appointed from London. With time, these colonies became more prosperous than the colonial state and saw a lot of immigration, especially of indentured servants. They were taken on contract basis and nearly half the European settlements were of this nature. The southern colonies were based on agriculture with slave labour coming from Africa which first began to arrive in 1612. By 1770, they formed 20% of the population.

These colonies enjoyed a lot of autonomy and did not have British laws strictly imposed on them. The French territories in Canada and Louisiana also became part of them. A Royal proclamation of 1763 organised these colonies while protecting the rights of the indigenous people in the central and western part.

The beginning of the resistance to the British colonial rule, following the defeat of the French, began after imposition of taxes beginning with the Stamp Act of 1765. One of the famous resistance to the tea tax was the Boston Tea Party of 1773. It was the first time the colonies organised themselves through two Continental Congress sessions but the colonial powers did not relent. It was also the first time that the seeds of civil rights and liberties were sown in and the people could not tolerate the Britishers trampling over these. Massachusetts saw armed conflict against these taxes in 1775. The Declaration of Independence was made on 4th July, 1776 with the content being to preserve the right to life, liberty and happiness. The concept of a Republic was embellished by the Founding Fathers.

While the war began in April, 1776, it went on for six years. The decisive victories for the Continental army were that of New York, New Jersey, Saratoga and Yorktown. The cessation of hostilities only happened in December 1782. After winning the war with the colonial power, the borders of the new nation were established in 1783 after the Paris Peace Treaty. The western parts of the country ceded to the Confederation. However, there were wars with the indigenous Indians who were also supported by the British.

The nationalists came together in each of the States and Philadelphia Convention was held in 1787. This sought to have a federal government. However, the British rule heightened the need for preserving individual rights and liberty. George Washington who played a pivotal role in the Confederate war against the colonial power became the first President and actually set the precedent of limiting the office to two terms. The Constitution came in 1788 and the Bill of Rights was adopted in 1791. The latter was the outcome of the idea for preservation of individual liberties in a strong central administrative setup. The two party system also emanated at this time with the Federalists under Washington and the Republicans under Jefferson. The former espoused commercial interests including good relations with Britain while the latter was skeptical of centralized power and wanted individual rights and liberties.

Washington was made the capital in 1800. After the Republicans under Jefferson came to power, Louisiana was purchased from France in 1803 thereby enlarging the US. It led to the westward expansion with the regime focussed more on the agriculturists and cultivators with skepticism of the central government, judiciary and industrial establishment.

The second war of independence was fuelled by the Britishers wanting to enlist Americans for the war against Napoleon. The former also supported the indigenous Indians with a view to create a buffer state to arrest the westward expansion and even threats to Canada. While the war itself was a stalemate, the Americans managed to repulse the threat from the Indians while the British burnt down Washington but tasted defeat at Baltimore and New Orleans. This war is said to have led to the demise of the anti-war Federalist party. The Republicans also split and the Democratic Party that emerged from it espoused the original principles of the Jefferson era. Another faction formed the Whigs Party.

The economic policies in the post war era were marked by imposition of tariffs as well as the closure of private banks. It was clearly inward looking and protectionist but the difficult circumstances warranted it. The foreign policy under the Monroe Doctrine was clear that they would not tolerate any interference from European powers.

The Indian Removal Act then sought the removal of the indigenous people from the eastern part of the country to settle in the unexplored west. It was a tragic phase as the Indians were removed against their wishes. The westward expansion towards the Pacific Coast began in search of land. The settlers in the west came into conflict with and defeated the indigenous people. It went on for a few decades. It was costly for both sides with an estimated 50,000 killed.

This expansion also resulted in a war with Mexico mainly over the regions of Texas and California. The Democrats supported this expansion and the war. They even wanted to capture the whole of Mexico but the White Southerners resisted this. The expansion was also fuelled by the California gold rush which saw the Mexican settlers called Hispanics overwhelmed resulting in a genocide. The Oregon trails also led to the capture of territory in the Northwestern part. As far as the islands were concerned, one of the drivers to capture these were the presence of guano which was a fertilizer.

However, slave labour remained a core area of division of this large country. The southern colonies continued to maintain that though the other states abolished it. The former's argument was that it benefited the slave labour themselves and would be economically fatal if removed. The New Republican Party emerged which wanted the abolishment of this practice. After Abraham Lincoln became President in 1860, seven southern states seceded in 1861 from the Union and formed the Confederacy. They attacked the US army base in South Carolina and got the support of four more states who seceded.

This resulted in the Civil War where the Confederate of Southern States were pitted against the forces of the Union. It was a bloody war with the Union Army heroes being General Sherman and Grant while the Confederates had General Lee. It was probably the first industrial war as railroads, communication lines, steamships and industrial mass produced weapons were part of the entire war strategy on both sides. The British true to their nature helped out both sides. Finally the Confederacy was defeated in 1865. The war took a heavy toll on the economy with more than a million people having perished and extensive damage to the infrastructure especially in the South.

Post war, slavery was abolished throughout the nation. However, in 1863, the Emancipation Proclamation was issued which recognized the 3 million slave labour in the South as free. However, not all of them could be freed until the defeat of the Confederacy in 1865.

Nevertheless, the white supremacy and discrimination continued to exist in the southern colonies. The ex-confederates continued to rule these States until there was political reorganisation. The Democrats got power in the southern states. It was the phase in which white supremist organisations like the Ku Klux Klan, White League and the Red Shirts tried to establish themselves but were not successful. The period from 1890 to 1908 was one of the dark phases for the rights of the blacks in the country with disenfranchise and discriminatory segregation laws being passed.

The last phase of the 19th century and the dawn of the 20th century saw the country industrialise. The economic growth was fuelled by immigrant workers and farmers. Railroad connection was established and a number of reforms undertaken until 1920. There were also allegations of corruption and unethical business practices as wealth and prosperity grew. It was the wave of mass immigration from Europe with estimates of around 22 million having migrated. It laid down the very base of the American principle of attracting the best talent around the world and continues to this day. However, there were phases of labour unrest as some railroad companies went through a difficult phase. President Mckinley came to power and initiated some reforms including having the gold standard and raising tariffs. Social reforms were also initiated such as women's suffrage as well as progressive changes in education and health.

As the nation became economically and militarily powerful, the imperialist ambitions surfaced. One of this was Philippines but there was little achieved there. They also looked at Cuba, Puerto Rico and Guam. Some of these were also driven by economic factors such as the need for opening of the Panama canal.

The country initially remained neutral in World War 1 under the leadership of President Woodrow Wilson. However, the sinking of the US ships supplying to the Allied Powers like the RMS Lusitania by German submarines was the trigger for entering the war in April 1917. The US played a critical role in the victory over the Axis. They also played a key role in the Versailles Treaty that was considered harsh on Germany. Many argue that this Treaty set the stage for the rise of the Nazis in Germany. However, the US never ratified the treaty.

While the 1920's were a period of tremendous growth and prosperity, the decade ended with the Great Depression of 1929. This was on account of a financial bubble of the stock markets which crashed later. There was increase in unemployment as well as falling manufacturing output and farm prices. The New Deals programme of Franklin Roosevelt which provided relief for workers and farmers helped the country come out of this Depression. There was a second Deals programme too in 1935-36 which provided another boost to the ailing economy.

The US once again maintained neutrality in World War II while tacitly supporting the Allied Powers in the fight against Nazi Germany. However, after the bombing of Pearl Harbour in a daring raid by the Japanese in 1941, they were forced to join it. They played a critical role in defeating the Nazis, liberating France after the Normandy landings and capturing key cities of Germany. During the war itself, the Manhattan project was going on which developed the nuclear bombs. They used the atomic weapons over Hiroshima and Nagasaki to force the Japanese to surrender. However, the US was less affected by the war than the other Allies given the geographical distance and less military losses. However, they had to give up Philippines.

The foreign policy in the phase was to contain the spread of communism and help out the European allies who were devastated after the war. They entered into a phase of a cold war with the Soviets and their allies. The NATO and the Warsaw pact came out of the result of this situation. It was an arms races along with development in other areas like space. It was this policy that triggered their entry into the Korean and Vietnamese wars. In 1960 when Kennedy became the president, the incidents that occurred were the Bay of Pigs and Cuban Missile crisis. Internally, the country went through a civil rights movement spearheaded by Martin Luther King. It led to the establishment of voting rights for the Afro Americans.

With the breakup of the Soviet Union in 1991, the country remained the sole superpower. The US intervened in many conflicts ranging from the Middle East. The war in Iraq and Afghanistan are the key ones. They also supported Ukraine in its conflict with Russia. The country has been using all opportunities to supply arms from its industry.

With the advent of China and its military build up, the overall power imbalance has been corrected. China continues to grow at a rapid pace and has become a superpower to contend with, replacing the erstwhile Soviet Union. The Trump administration was the first one to take measures to contain China including supporting countries who had bilateral disputes with the latter.

With a history of racism with the civil war being fought on slave trade, it has not been an easy transition. The country has also had immigration issues from the south namely Mexico and other Central American countries. As for the other immigrants, the filters have ensured adequate screening. Compared to Europe, the economic status of this set of immigrants has been relatively better off.

The history of the country specifically its dominance at the world stage has what has shaped its behaviour. Their bureaucracy and diplomats have been moulded to be arrogant and talk down upon others. This behaviour is manifested in the way they speak without any diplomatic niceties. Basically, they do not mince words and are brutally frank in their expressions. However, the citizens have a good commercial perspective and are thus come straight to the point of their commercial interest. They prefer to deal with the core matter and keep meetings short and crisp. They do not believe in beating around the bush and dwell on unrelated issues before coming to the matter at hand. Therefore, it may be difficult to deal with them and many would portray them as being brash and ruthless.

On the other hand, the relationship with other communities like the blacks and the Hispanics does have elements of racism. But the economic status of these communities is much better than in the rest of the developed world where they are in minority.

****

CHAPTER EIGHTEEN

The Regional Satraps

Another grouping of countries are those who aspire to be or are actually regional powerhouses. The thinking which precipitated this regional dominance has been moulded by their history too. Circumstances such as their size, military strength, economic might and geo-political circumstances.

It's a different matter that some of them were also colonial powers but did not achieve the type of dominance or leave the imprint of their culture on the colonies like some of the others colonisers. However, there was always the aspiration to exercise regional hegemony, both with a view to expanding influence and even in the case of existentialism.

These nations exert influence in their regions, not just through military muscle. It has been their economic growth which has made them significant players and earned them the right to flaunt their regional powerhouse status. The military buildup has been one of the tools to exert an influence in the region. It is a double whammy in that it ensures self defence as also scares away potential adversaries. On the economic front, the regional satraps have focussed on some core strengths and leveraged these. Investments and trade have also been routes to ensure this economic build up.

The behaviour of these nations is influenced by their history. Some of them have learnt from their past and adapted to the new world order. Some others have progressed beyond anyone's imagination through the dint of hard and smart work.

These regional satraps have also become a model for many other nations as they exert influence in their domains. Let us look at their history and understand how their behaviour has evolved?

****

• 91 •

CHAPTER NINETEEN

Singapura

The island city is today the economic envy of the entire ASEAN region despite its size. Its transition is an amazing story from the times when it part of the Malay kingdom and then unceremoniously kicked out to be a free nation. Today, it has left its parent far behind as far as global clout and economic power are concerned.

The earliest mention of this country is from the 2nd – 3rd century both by the Greek astronomer Ptolemy as well as in a Chinese book. The Chola kings of India are supposed to have attacked and controlled this place around 1025 AD.

Even during the 14th century, it is documented to have been a trading point given its strategic location at the tip of the Malay peninsula. These were based on reports of emissaries of the Mongols as well as Chinese travellers. Evidence suggests that it was ruled by Parameshwara, the King of Singapura and was part of the Malacca Sultanate. The entry of the Portuguese further led to the capture of Malacca and the sultan escaped southwards to Singapore in the 16th century. It subsequently became part of the Johor Sultanate. The Dutch has also imprinted themselves and the Sultanate was under their control. The Portuguese then destroyed the island and nothing was known of it in the next two centuries until the Britishers came.

Stamford Raffles, a Britisher negotiated a treaty with the Johor Sultanate to locate a trading port on the island in 1819. This was done to reduce the influence of other powers like the Dutch as well as the need for a new port for trade between China and India. His successor Crawford signed a second treaty in 1823 with the Sultan and the country came under the control of the East India company in 1824. A treaty was also signed with Dutch in the same year which gave British the rights over Singapore. With its strategic location, it became an important route of trade between China and Europe. Beginning with a population of 1000, it slowly expanded on account of the migration of the Chinese, Malays and Indians with these communities forming the bulk of the population of the island. Many of these workers came for the plantations and tin mines too.

The opening of the Suez Canal in 1869 provided a further boost to trade and established the importance of Singapore. The absence of taxation made it an entrepot trading hub replacing all the other competitors in the region including Jakarta and Manila which had customs duties.

However, the administration which was run by the British from India was ineffective. There were violent inter gang rivalries, health services were abysmal in the light of outbreaks and drug abuse was rampant. It was then that the Crown colony of Singapore was established in 1867 with the presence of a governor for better administration. The administration looked at improving the services for its population, most of who were Chinese immigrants, addressing health issues and banning of secret societies.

The only major incident that happened during World War 1 was a mutiny by British Indian Muslim soldiers when they heard of rumours of being sent to fight the Ottoman Empire. This revolt was quickly suppressed. Post war, the threat of the Japanese empire forced Britain to build a naval base but the British fleet was not stationed there.

It was occupied by the Japanese in February 1942 until the end of World War II. The capitulation was unexpected as Britain expected a naval attack from the south and had stationed two of its frigates *"Prince of Wales"* and *"Repulse"*, both of which were sunk by the Japanese in an aerial bombardment. The Japanese used light tanks to overrun Malay from the north and attacked Singapore. It was an abject surrender by the British garrison and is one of their most ignominious defeats of the war. The Japanese mistreated all section of the society namely the Chinese, Indians and Malays. The forced labour for building the Thailand-Myanmar railway line led to the deaths of many of the prisoners of war.

Subsequently, it reverted to British control after the war but denigrated to a period of violence, riots and loot. The infrastructure was in a pitiable state and the credibility of the Britishers had been tarnished with their abject surrender to Japan. It led to the awakening of anti-colonial sentiments. A model of self-governance was established until its merger with Malaysia in 1963. This merger was preceded by a referendum. Nevertheless, due to political differences, racial tensions and social unrest, it was literally kicked out by Malaysia whose Parliament voted unanimously to remove Singapore from the federation. It thus became independent much against its own wishes in 1965.

At the time of independence, it was beset with problems of unemployment and lack of housing and health. However, it established a credible foreign policy and even co-founded the Association of East Asian Nations or ASEAN in August, 1967. Its economic development fuelled by the leadership of Lee Kuan Yew then began and made it a prosperous economy centred around trade and tourism. In one of his famous quotes he said, *"My main mission when I became Prime Minister, was to keep Singapore going and Singapore has been kept going."*

This was on account of industrial estates in Jurong focusing on petrochemicals and chemicals as well as the service sector fuelled by the shipping industry and finance. It also became a hub for civil aviation with the Singapore Airlines being one of the premier airlines of the world. The tourism industry has also got a fillip with the establishment of the Sentoso resort and the Marina Sands Bay casino. It became the 7th largest economy even surpassing Malaysia.

However, while elections are held on a regular basis in the country, it has been a one party rule namely the People's Action Party. The country is ruled with a firm hand. The Party decided that for hard decisions to be taken for economic progress, democratic institutions could not be given a free hand. Discipline including facets of law and order, cleanliness and adherence to strong work ethics has been the crux of how its administration is run.

Its economic prosperity had led it to flex its muscles in the East Asian region. It is believed to exercise a lot of control, almost like a mafia, in the working of ASEAN despite being the smallest country in size. This has also generated a lot of arrogance in the way it deals with the developing countries. Moreover, the money power has also reflected in their overall attitude. With the Chinese community controlling the business in the region and the Malays having a lot of reservation in the political space, it is the Indians and the others in general who are probably at the lower end of the economic stratum.

Therefore, in the historical context, the country was ruled by various Sultanates before coming under colonial rule. Its strategic location at the tip of the Malay peninsula made it ideal for being a trading entrepot. The British rule with the capitulation in World War II and the subsequent Japanese rule raised anti-colonial sentiments. After being kicked out by Malaysia from the federation, the disciplined leadership then transformed the nation into an economic power. All this has seeped into the level of self confidence sometimes bordering on arrogance. The behavioural pattern today is an outcome of these historical events.

In terms of behaviour, one can expect them to be condescending towards others, specifically developing countries. In the ASEAN grouping, they exercise a lot of clout and strangely even the large countries like Indonesia, Malaysia and Thailand remain cowed down by them in various facets like trade negotiations. It is money that talks and they have used it effectively to enhance their clout. They have a shrewd business sense and have made the country an economic powerhouse in the region.

****

CHAPTER TWENTY

Deutschland

While, it has been the military and economic engine of Europe, Germany became infamous after its role in the two World Wars which it lost. Nevertheless, it has in a way buried its ignominious past and re-emerged as an economic powerhouse of the region. However, it is important to understand how the country evolved in the run up to the war itself.

The Germanic tribes occupied the region around the Rhine river and around 9AD repulsed attacks from the Roman empire to take it over. Ironically, most of the settlers in Europe including their traditional adversaries like France and UK are descendants of these Germanic tribes. Subsequently, the Franks occupied this region and during the division in 843AD, it became part of East Francia. Finally, in the struggles, it became part of the Holy Roman Empire at the end of the first millenium.

During the middle of the second millenium, the Hanseatic League was established in the northern part with the port cities of the Baltics which later became the region of Prussia. The middle age period also saw the mushrooming of powerful regional satraps like bishops, dukes and princes which challenged the Roman emperor. 1517 also saw the Protestant Reformation of Martin Luther thus leading to the division of the church itself. While the North and East became largely protestant, the South and West retained Catholicism.

The civil war of 1618 also known as the Thirty Years War led to greater autonomy for the provinces of Austria, Bavaria, Prussia and Saxony. These wars also destroyed the Holy Roman Empire and was eventually dissolved in 1806. Napolean established the Confederation of the Rhine within the French empire but was eventually defeated. The German Confederation was eventually established under Austrian Presidency. There were revolutions in 1848-49 but could not unite the region. Nevertheless, the industrial revolution modernized the country and ensured development of its science and arts too.

Eventually, the unification of the German Federation was brought about in 1871 by Chancellor Otto Von Bismarck. The stage was also set for the colonial expansion, chiefly in Africa and the Pacific. It developed its navy which was supposedly more powerful than that of Britain. However, in World War 1, it led the Central Powers but lost. Subsequently, the revolution led to the abdication of the emperor and the formation of the Weimar Republic. While this was a parliamentary democracy, it was unstable.

The interwar period saw a lot of disenchantment within Germany in what was perceived to be a lopsided Versailles Treaty that had enervated the once strong nation and made them lose territory. The German nationalists jumped into the fray eager to leverage this seething anger and propagated Lebensraum, a concept used by geographers justifying the need for space.

The humiliation of the war and the reparations thereof was utilized by Adolf Hitler, the leader of the Nazi party to whip up emotions and lay forth his expansionist plans. The three pronged rationale as also expounded in Hitler's "*Mein Kampf*" were the need to restore lost pride, overpopulation which required lands for settlement and provision of natural resources for the country to flourish. They also propagated the racial superiority of the Germanic people over the slavics in Eastern Europe namely Ukraine, Poland and Russia. The entire war was sold to the German people on this theory. This deadly concoction is what brainwashed the population and the Nazis started their operations eastwards attacking Czechoslovakia.

Ironically, Hitler in his autobiography had also painted a positive picture of the American westward expansion which had led to the genocide of the indigenous Red Indians. The grabbing of lands in this westward expansion was another source of inspiration for the Fuhrer. The dependency on food imports during World War 1 was used as a pretext for territorial expansion which led to the capture of swathes of fertile land in Eastern Europe which could then act as food bowls for the Germans.

The aim was to establish the Great German Reich which would rule over a thousand years. The main target was Russia since it provided the agricultural land and natural resources for the German state. The racist intent was also to keep the German bloodline pure and purge it off the other nationalities. It was tantamount to ethnic cleansing of many of the communities of non-Germanic origin, chiefly the Jews. Strangely, the Nazis also differentiated between different strands of non-Germans. For them, those in Western Europe and Scandinavia could still co-exist with Germans but the rest of the territories that they intended to occupy were placed on a different pedestal with a view to being discriminated in all walks of life.

The Nazis were quite successful in implementing Lebensraum in the first couple of years of the war. Their tank formation known as the Panzers and the air force called the Luftwaffe managed to steamroll along the mainland capturing France and reaching to the outskirts of the major Soviet cities like Leningrad, Moscow and Stalingrad. However, defeat by the Soviet forces at all the three cities turned the tide of the war from which they could never recover. The heroics of the Red Army as they eroded the confidence of the German military was the catalyst for the defeat of the Nazis. The fall of Berlin and the suicide of Hitler ended their infamy in 1945.

After the war, Germany was split among the Allied powers like Britain, France and US who administered West Germany while the Soviets administered East Germany. The former had a democratic set up while the latter was communist. The levels of development also varied. Both countries grew up in their own systems with the Berlin wall exemplifying the differences in their systems. However, with time the demand for integration became vocal and with the perestroika in the Soviet Union, the wall fell in 1989. With the Soviet Union disintegrating, the unification of Germany was inevitable but the transition was painful especially for the communist east.

However, post war, the real will power of the denizens of this land came forth. Rather than brooding over the destruction of their land, they rebuilt it to become the biggest powerhouse of Europe. Of course, a lot of funding came from the Allies who had defeated them in the war. Moreover, a strong bond was forged with the French and these two became the fulcrum of the European Union, a grouping created with one of the geo-strategic goals being of not getting into any further mess which instigated the two world wars.

Coming to the behavioural aspects of the Germans, there is no doubt that the chequered history of the world wars made them the villians of the world. After having shaken the yolk of the Roman Empire and the French rulers, they embarked on the path of colonial expansionism. The concept of Lebensraum which the Germans bought into during the Nazi rule clearly showed their racist tendencies, in part driven by the treatment meted out to them after the loss in World War I. The persecution of the Jews would ever go down in their log books as a blot which is difficult to be effaced. But many argue that they have recovered from this chequered phase of their history and have now become the economic powerhouse of Europe. As for the people, they are probably closer to being arguably the most forthright folks in the continent. Basically, not meandering around with their words and action. Quite like the Americans who like to come to the point, especially in business deals without beating around the bush. This could also lead to some impatience and possibility of avoiding wasting of time in niceties. The *condescending attitude and one laced in racism*" would definitely continue when dealing with people from developing countries. The history of the wars has something to do with it. The society is also highly disciplined which made them overcome all the adversities and recoup from the devastating wars to become the powerhouse of Europe.

****

CHAPTER TWENTY-ONE

Developing Nations

The developing nations are the ones who while being rich in resources could never attain the commensurate level of economic development. One of the key reasons was the economic impoverishment due to the colonial rule which drained their wealth.

Some of them had a rich history wherein there were many civilizations that flourished. They were very wealthy during some of these dynastic rules primarily due to the availability of resources, economic growth premised on specific sectors such as agriculture and overall good governance. However, it was this very wealth that proved to be their undoing as they were unable to withstand the onslaught of colonial powers and succumbed quite meekly. They were unable to have a viable military force nor could they stand united in the face of adversity.

The colonial rule in most cases enervated them and left them languishing in the lower end of the economic spectrum. Finally, the rule also broke their mental spirit as they believed they were inferior to their colonial masters.

However, after the colonial rule, things started perking up with control back in their hands. The historical evolution of these countries prior to the colonial rule in a way reflects their attitude. Certain adaptions did occur during the colonial rule which in a way led to the final moulding of their behaviour.

We would pick up some countries in this basket who have now shown remarkable progress. They dominate the continents where they reside. Most of them are slowly blossoming out of the mental indoctrination that they went through during the colonial rule.

****

CHAPTER TWENTY-TWO

Rainbow Nation

South Africa is known as the cradle of mankind as the first humans are supposed to have inhabited this country around 100,000 years back. The first migration of the Bantus from central and western Africa occurred around 1000BC as they mixed with the original denizens like the Khoisan, Khoikhoi, Khwe and San. There was even the Mapungubwa kingdom between 900-1300 AD which controlled the trade routes to China, India and Persia.

Portuguese were the first Europeans who set foot in West Africa during the 13th century ostensibly to look at alternate routes to China. They explored the continent and by the end of the 15th century had mapped the Cape of Good Hope. Vasco de Gama sailed around the Cape and even reached India thus finding a new route between Asia and Europe.

The Dutch East India Company or VOC then came and settled down in Cape Town around the middle of the 17th century. The initial purpose was to service trading ships on route to Asia but gradually they brought in Dutch farmers known as free burghers who expanded their settlements. Subsequently, people of German and French origin also settled here. They also got slave labour from India, Indonesia, Madagascar, Mauritius, and East Asia for the settlements. The VOC had a war with the indigenous Khoikhois who were driven out of the Cape region. Subsequently, during the end of the 19th century, they also explored the interiors and came in touch with the Bantu people. There were some skirmishes with these indigenous people over land and cattle.

By the end of the 19th century, the Britishers came to the country and this forced the Dutch settlers to migrate inland and establish Boer Republics. The Dutch were paid 6 million pounds for the colony after which the sovereignty of the British was recognised. The latter had initially come to thwart French takeover after they had defeated the Dutch back home. They too looked at it as a strategic port for passage into India only but slowly established their hegemony.

The various indigenous tribes like the Zulus then witnessed consolidation. They established a kingdom under the leadership of Shaka after the union of the various clans. This was also necessitated by the European colonial powers who were establishing themselves in the continent. It was a disciplined force which managed to expand. However, in the succession battles, they were weakened and defeated by the British. There were fights with the other indigenous people by both the Dutch settlers and the British as it was a struggle for land. These were the Griquas who fought with the Orange State, Xhosas in the South Eastern part of the country, Basathos in the Lower Caledon Valley, Ndebele in the northwestern part and the Bapedi on the border with Swaziland.

The Britishers did replace Dutch language with English. However, they continued with the Roman Dutch law and preserved the rights of the people in the colonies. There were tensions with the settlers over the compensation paid to them for freeing the slave labour that they got from distant lands. This was what forced the Dutch settlers to migrate to the interiors. They did get a large number of immigrants from the homeland during 1820. These migrants settled down in Grahamstown and Port Elizabeth.

This migration of Dutch settlers was what led to the formation of the Boer Republics around the region, especially during the latter half of the 19th century. Some of these included the Republics of Transvaal, Orange Free State and Natalia. They depended largely on slave labour. The Cape Colony remained as the original British settlement.

The discovery of gold and diamonds in the interiors changed the entire economic landscape of the region with mining becoming a key activity. Diamond was discovered around 1866 in and around Kimberley while gold deposits were found in 1886. The diamond and gold magnates such as Cecil Rhodes and Charles Rudd made a beeline for the scramble into the continent. Labour initially came from the indigenous people but later on even the Chinese labourers were settled around these mines. Disenchantment was also rife on account of the absence of voting rights for the British managers and engineers of the mines who were being controlled by Dutch supervisors. The British empire also seized this opportunity and waged war against the Boer states and even the indigenous people. It was a war for primarily for control over the mines. In the first Anglo-Boer war, the British were repulsed and the Boer republics formed a loose coalition. However, in the second war, the Britishers regrouped with reinforcements from their colonies and outnumbered their adversaries. It was a bloody battle with Boers surrendering by 1902. It is estimated that the casualties were around 50,000 while the British concentration camps had appalling conditions leading to more deaths. The Boer wars led to the British establishing their foothold in the country. The country was made into a Union in 1910 with the amalgamation of all the colonies of the Cape, Natal, Orange River and Transvaal.

The most pernicious aspect during the British rule was that they practiced racial discrimination. The most famous incident being that of Mahatma Gandhi being thrown out of a train in Petermaritzburg in 1893. After the formation of the Union, laws excluded the blacks from voting and gave them only 7% of the total land. 20% of the white population held 90% of the land. In a way, these policies also kept the Boers under check by easing the racial tensions between the descendants of the Dutch known as Afrikaners and those of British ancestry.

The country had a key role in both World War 1 and II. The strategic location for the British navy as well as attacks on the German colonies in Africa were undertaken. However, there was sympathy towards Germany since they had supplied weapons during the Boer war for resisting the British. This translated into a rebellion during World War 1 which was suppressed. Some of the parties that came up post World War II were also pro Nazi in their outlook.

The monarchy ended in May 1961 and it became a Republic. However, the most ignominious phase of the country was the apartheid policy from 1948 until its dismantling in 1994. It was a racist policy that discriminated against both the brown and black skinned people. It was a continuation of the Dutch policy and percolated into the British rule too. There were policies to have reserves for the indigenous people. The United Nations also passed a resolution in 1966 which was opposed by Portugal, South Africa, UK and US. However, despite the UN imposing an arms embargo, the country had close military ties with Israel and managed to equip its military.

The African National Congress (ANC) fought tooth and nail against this heinous policy and its most famous leader Nelson Mandela was jailed. The struggle was both peaceful inspired by Mahatma Gandhi's ideology as well as armed. The latter included attacks on military and political targets. The massacre of peaceful demonstrators in Sharpville was one of the triggers for the transition to armed resistance. The sanctions against the apartheid regime did not improve the situation and actually further impoverished the victims of this regime.

Finally, the regime came to an end in 1994 and a government of unity was formed. It was a difficult transition and credit to its first premier Nelson Mandela that he managed to make his cabinet inclusive and prevented any backlash against the perpetrators of the apartheid policy. The ANC has been in power ever since. However, the modern country has been beset with problems of unemployment, rising crime, corruption and poor infrastructure.

South Africa is a mixture of various cultures and hence the behavioural traits vary. However, its history which saw the conflicts with the indigenous people and the apartheid regime deeply influences its thought process. Racial undertones remain among its white population whose ancestors were given special privileges in the apartheid history. On the other hand, the brown population of South Asian origin are caught in between with some still seeing themselves as victims of the discrimination policies of yore. The black population however, still harbour a lot of resentment since the post apartheid South Africa hasn't yet fulfilled the aspirations and dreams that were nurtured.

Given its multicultural society, there is still a lot of empathy towards the people from developing countries. However, each segment of the population has a different behavioural trait. The whites still harbouring a feeling of racial superiority despite the dismantling of the apartheid regime while the blacks still carrying the feeling of victimization. It is thus a complex behavioural pattern and one needs to suitably tailor the responses.

****

CHAPTER TWENTY-THREE

Samba country

Samba country, the beautiful game; pretty beaches and the vast pristine Amazon forests. These are the general perceptions of this vast country called Brazil. While its history may not be as old and varied as the rest of the world, it does carry with it the remnants of the behaviour of its denizens.

While traces of early civilization date back to around 11,000 years, it is believed to have been inhabited by around two thousand diverse tribes when the Portuguese set foot on it. They were primarily hunters, food gatherers and did some primitive farming in the lands. Most of them lived around the coast or the along the banks of its big rivers. However, there is little written records of these civilisations since there was no documentation. Archeological excavations point to development of pottery.

Pedro Cabral, the first Portuguese explorer reached the country in 1500 while on a mission to find India. In the three centuries thereafter, it was expanded and made part of the Portuguese empire. The name translated into *"Land of the Holy Cross"* also got its origin from the brazilwood found in its forests. This wood was treasured for the red dye extracted from it.

The settlers introduced crops like coffee, oranges, rice, sugar, tobacco and wheat along with animal husbandry, stonemasonry and metal working. However, the sugar plantations were the primary reason why slave labour was brought from Africa. There was an attempt to use indigenous people to work but many of them escaped to the jungles. Hence the dependency on imported labour was felt. Brazil became one of the major producers of sugar during this period. Some of the other colonial powers like the Dutch and the French also tried to establish bases and grow these crops. However, the Portuguese managed to drive them out. A diverse culture with inter-marriages was also created due to the influx of immigrants from Africa and other regions.

Gold was yet another commodity that changed the economic face of Brazil. These were found around the Minas Gerais region. It was a windfall for Portugal that used it to trade in other commodities like textiles as well as build monuments back home. Arms were also purchased through it. A lot of slave labour was employed for extraction from the mines. Despite the presence of a large number of Portuguese officials, they were unable to have an effective regulatory framework for it. It was only after the independence of Brazil that British companies like Rey Mining company came in and adopted modern engineering management practices. Diamonds were also found in the region and there was a rush to control its mining too. It also added to the wealth of the colonial power.

Coffee was also a major plantation crop of the region after being introduced in 1720. The country had half the world production by the middle of the 19th century. While the workers were from Africa, there were immigrants from Italy, Japan and Spain who managed the plantations. On the other hand, the rubber boom occurred around the Amazon and transformed the region at the end of the 19th century and early 20th century. Manaus was the centre of this boom but this ended in 1920.

There were skirmishes with the indigenous people, many of whom formed coalitions such as the Tamayo Confederation in the middle of the 16th century. One of the objectives of this rebellion was also against the slave labour who were settled in the lands. The Portuguese managed to quell these rebellions.

With the colonial conquest of lands in Africa and the Americas; Portugal and Spain entered into the Treaty of Tordesillas in 1494. The lands east of Cape Verde islands were given to Spain while those west of it were in Portuguese hand. This Treaty was the basis on which Brazil came under colonial rule of the Portugal and the other powers did not interfere. It was also the basis on which the Dutch were driven out of the country.

The conditions of slave labour were inhuman and many of them were subject to torture. This was what led to the famous rebellion by Zumbi in the region of Pernambuco. However, after an intense struggle, the Portuguese firepower was too much to handle and he was captured and hung. It was a message sent to others who were disenchanted with the treatment of slave labourers.

Prior to the independence of the country, the Portuguese monarchy had fled in 1809 and taken refuge in the country due to the Napoleonic wars that affected Portugal. The monarchy remained till 1821 before the king returned to his home country but left his eldest son back to rule. Independence was won in 1822 with support of the monarchy and the Brazilian empire was established. The monarchy continued till 1889 before being overthrown by inspiration from the French revolution.

In 1889, it became a Presidential Republic after a military coup. However, the period after this was a roller coaster ride with military rules, democracies, oligarchies ruling it in various phases. The foreign policy was isolationalist with brief phases of alignment with the West. While its role in World War I was limited, it sided with the Allies in World War II. There was a phase of military government from 1964 until 1989 after which the country became a democratic republic. The military regime had been accused of crimes against both the population and the indigenous people.

The large country is characterized by social and economic inequality. At one end of the spectrum are the slums of Rio de Janeiro while at the other are the millionaire farmers who have helicopters to go from one part of their ranch to the other. The social inequality has also festered crime. Some of the street snatching incidents during the Rio Olympics were a testimony to this.

The economy has done reasonably well under the democratic rule. It has become the most powerful Latin American nation leveraging its natural resources, agricultural productivity and rich human resources. Its industrial sector has also done well in specific sectors like engineering and automotives. The services sector has also performed reasonably well.

As far as behavioural aspects are concerned, they are very warm, social and fun loving. Friendships are easily made. The quote "*A life lived in Brazil is a life lived for relationships,*" personifies the character of the people and their tethering with family roots. Moreover, they tend to be more relaxed and take life easy. Probably a typical latino trait. The economic boom has been beneficial to the wealthy and there is huge disparity. It's a good country to go business with. The levels of trust are higher than many others.

****

CHAPTER TWENTY-FOUR

Rich civilisations

We come to the last set of countries, all of which had an ancient civilization steeped in rich culture and heritage. These had a profound effect on the denizens of those civilisations and their behaviour. Most of these civilisations grew up on the back of good administrative and governance structures. Law and order was an important aspect which enabled rulers to exercise their authority.

There were a number of factors that contributed to the establishment of these civilisations. These were the feasible geographical location which included river valleys, entrepot junction for trade and creation of social structures which led to efficient distribution of capital and labour. Agriculture became the main stay of these civilisations since it was important to satiate the food demand of the population. It was only then that the focus could be on other activities like architecture, arts, culture etc.

The causality of these civilizations with the behaviour of its present people is a matter of speculation. There is no doubt that they are proud of their rich cultural heritage. But do they relate to it in their real life is not very clear. Nevertheless, these civilizations provides a level of confidence to the people with the fact that it could be replicated at a higher level taking into account the modern means.

However, subsequent to the fall of these civilisations, many of these nations fell prey to succession battles. They disintegrated and were even susceptible to invasions. Some of them became part of other empires and much of the civilization traits were lost.

Therefore, there were disruptive forces at play well before the advent of colonization. The colonial powers however tried to change the very cultural ethos of these countries. They tried their best to instill a fear of inferiority complex so as mentally break them down. The primary motive was to ensure that the citizens of these countries remained subservient and were not proud of their historical past. This worked well in many cases and helped suppress any dissent.

Hence, the behaviour of these nations is quite complex. An admixture of the ancient civilizational traits, the post civilization anarchy, rule by other empires or colonial powers and finally the evolution of the modern state.

****

CHAPTER TWENTY-FIVE

The Land of the Pharoahs

Egypt has been associated with the rich and ancient civilization along the banks of its lifeline, the Nile river. Starting at around 3150BC, the ancient Egyptian dynasty is believed to have ruled until 600BC before being overun by the Achaemenid empire of Persia.

In 332BC, Alexander the Great conquered Egypt and made it part of the Macedonian empire. However, this was short lived as rebellions led to its weakening and it was finally conquered by the Roman empire with Cleopatra being the last queen of Egypt. It was part of the Roman empire from 30BC until 650 AD.

After this period came the advent of Islam. The Caliphates that ruled this country included the Rashidun, Umayyad, Abassid, Fatamid, Ayyumid and Mamluk. After this in 1517, the Ottoman empire overran the country and ruled over it. It remained part of this empire until the British controlled it in 1882.

The Kingdom of Egypt was formed in 1919 after the revolution. However, Britain continued to hold sway over foreign affairs and defence. The Kingdom was involved in the first Arab-Israel conflict of 1948 wherein they lost territories earmarked for the Arab state to Israel. However, the Sinai was retained as Egyptian territory. This lasted till 1954 as the British withdrew from the Suez Canal and the Republic was formed.

Under the Presidency of Gamel Nasser from 1956 until 1970, the country witnessed some reforms. It was part of the founding Members of the Non Aligned Movement or NAM which took a neutral role in the cold war. However, the six day war in June 1967 with Israel was the low point of Nasser's tenure. The relations with Israel had plummeted due to the occupation of the Palestine lands in the West Bank and Gaza strip. The war was however triggered by denial of shipping access to Israeli ships through the Suez Canal. In the first phase of this war, the Egyptian air force was immobilized by Israeli firepower which struck pre-emptively. After this, the Israeli forces occupied the Sinai peninsula and inflicted a decisive defeat on the Arab coalition led by Egypt. The Golan heights of Syria was also occupied since it was strategically located.

Then during the tenure of the Anwar Saddat, there was another war in 1973 which was launched on Yom Kippur day to take back both the Sinai peninsula and the Golan heights. After the initial success of the joint Arab forces based on their surprise attack, the Israelis struck back and managed to defend both the territories and push back both Egypt and Syria. They also made inroads coming close to both Cairo and Damascus. Thus the war was a stalemate. In the peace treaty, Sinai peninsula was returned to Egypt.

Mr Hosni Mubarak ruled the country for 30 years until he was deposed in the revolution of 2011. The main reasons for the revolution were the economic recession coupled with unemployment. The country has been through a tough phase ever since with changes of government.

In terms of the behavioural pattern, the Egyptians are warm and social. Relationships are built up over a period of time. They are good businessmen given their history as a trading centre.

****

CHAPTER TWENTY-SIX

Persia

Iran, historically known also as Persia began its journey nearly 6,000 years back with the first traces of civilization. There is evidence related to habitation during the Paleolithic, Neolithic, Chalcolithic, Bronze Age and Iron Age. It was ruled by the Kassites, Mannaeans, Gutians before the Medes unified the country in 625 BC.

The Achaeminid empire from 550-330BC and founded by Cyrus the Great had probably the largest expanse of any empire from the region. However, this was preceded by the Assyrians and Medes who waged internal battles for control of this territory. Cyrus united all these into his empire. His son conquered Egypt which was also made part of the empire. The empire had battles with the Greeks too but despite some territorial gains, they could not conquer the latter. Persian was developed as the lingua franca of the region around this period It was also the most prosperous phase in the history of the land.

Alexander the Great had conquered the region in 334BC and his general Seleucus had established the Seleucid empire. It was during this period that Greek was spoken. The Parthians came in 248BC and after defeating the Seleucid empire, were engaged in a war with the Romans. It lasted until 224AD when the Sasanians took over. They conquered a number of territories stretching in an east west expanse from Georgia to Pakistan and a north south expanse from Azerbaijan to Israel. They were involved in a war of attrition with the Byzantines. The Empire was a power centre comparable to that of the Roman and the subsequent Byzantine empires. However, there were invasions by the Macedonians too. The period of the Sassanians which went over four hundred years was considered the golden period of economic and military growth. However, they did wage war with the Byzantines and Roman empires. After the decisive defeat of the Roman empire in 260AD, they expanded to conquer Egypt, Jordan, Lebanon and Palestine. It was during the reign of the Sassanians that the term Eranshahr was used for the country. After some mixed results, they were defeated by the Byzantines in 632AD. The period also saw the flourishing of arts and culture of the region.

Islam came to the region with the fall of the Sasanian empire in 633 AD which eventually ended in 651AD by the slaying of the last king. The religion became the most widespread as it replaced Zorastrianism. It was the beginning of the Ummayad dynasty which initially adopted many of the erstwhile Persian customs and traditions. Eventually, Arabic was adopted as the official language at the end of the 7th century. The Ummayads were replaced by the Abbasids in 750AD and they adopted a more inclusive and multi-ethnic approach. Subsequently, the Samanid dynasty and the Ghaznawids saw the revival of Persian culture. The latter even conquered parts of the Indian sub-continent and introduced Islam to the region.

The Mongol invasion happened during the reign of Khwarazmian dynasty in 1219. Genghis Khan's troops had used Chinese gunpowder as a new weapon to overcome the Persians. The Mongols did not rule for long but their tenure caused immense destruction of the Islamic culture and its infrastructure. The remnants of the Mongol rulers established the Ikhanates which in a way morphed into a new Persian culture affected by the opening of trade routes to China and India.

After a period of instability caused by internal rivalries, the Timurid dynasty was established in 1381 with the invasion of Timur. It was a bloody confrontation that led to many deaths but it also saw the emergence of Sufism, which hitherto was discouraged by the earlier rulers.

However, the unification of the country happened in 1501 as the Safavid dynasty ruled the country which is considered as the era of modern Iran. The dynasty also made the country a force to reckon with becoming a rival to the Ottoman Empire. It had a vast territory ranging from Afghanistan, Armenia, Azerbaijan, Kuwait, Pakistan, Syria, Tajikistan, Turkmenistan and Uzbekistan. The country also had a monarchy which existed until 1979 It was at this point that Shia Islam became the official religion thus making it a centre of this sect of Islam. One of the greatest ruler was Shah Abbas 1 who reinforced the control over Georgia and also took the help of the Europeans chiefly the Dutch East India Company and the British to establish his firm grip on the empire.

However, the dynasty saw its end around 1722 as the subsequent rulers showed little interest in governance. The country became militarily weak. The Afghan rulers, Ottomans and the Russian empires exploited this vacuum by seizing territories and eventually dividing Persia among themselves.

However, Nadir Shah a warlord briefly restored the power of the Safavid dynasty. He assumed power and managed to unite much of the country. However, his most talked about accomplishment is the attack on the Mughal empire and the ransacking of Delhi whereby he looted its wealth and took it back to Persia. He also defeated the Ottomans, and Uzbeks. However, the guerrilla warfare by the Lezgins of Dagestan was what eventually led to his defeat. Soon Persia became fragmented after the defeat of the Zand kings that succeeded Nadir Shah.

However, Aga Khan of the Qajar dynasty managed to conquer Georgia, who sought Russian help which did not come. After the death of the Georgian ruler, the Persian Russian wars occurred during the 19th century. It led to the country losing a lot of its Caucasian territories such as Armenia, Azerbaijan, Dagestan and East Georgia to the Russian empire. Most of the Caucasian Muslims also escaped to Persia.

The Shah regime was the final phase of the Qajar dynasty which saw interface with the west. There were revolts against the regime but they managed to hang on granting limited constitutional powers. With the discovery of oil in 1908, the country became an epicentre for struggle between Britain and Russia. The country remained neutral in World War 1.

Subsequently in 1925, the Pahlavi dynasty took over and ruled till 1979. The first ruler Reza Shah introduced a number of reforms including making the state secular and modernizing it. However, this led to resentment from many who considered it an affront on Islam.

During World War 2, the region was occupied by the Soviet Red Army who used it as a conduit for supplying oil. This was on account of the oil rich Caucasian region coming under threat from the Nazis. After the war, the country was unstable and there was a coup against Mosaddeq by the Americans. The former was nationalizing the oil industry which rankled the western powers. This was probably the first intervention by the US which created bad blood between the two nations that lasts even till today.

After the success of the coup, the Shah dynasty usurped all powers and ruled the country. The regime was propped up by the west and initiated wide reforms and modernization. However, the core issue was the Iranian oil over which the west managed to wrest control through the Shah regime. Even the profits that were shared with the Iranian government were non transparent. This was what further sowed the seed of distrust of the west. It was only in 1973 that the oil industry was nationalized. Hence, despite the reforms, there was internal dissention fuelled by the draining of oil resources, atrocities of the secret police known as SAVAK as well as the social freedom which many religious hardliners interpreted as going against the tenet of Islam.

The Iranian revolution of 1979 marked a turning point for the country. There were demonstrations culminating in the fighting with the forces loyal to the Shah regime being defeated and the military remaining neutral. The country became an Islamic

Republic from this point on with Ayatollah Khomeni being the supreme leader. The regime completely changed Iranian society with industries nationalized with culture and education made Islamic.

It also led to the isolation of the country, especially from the west. The holding of American diplomats as hostages in 1979-81 further strained the relations between the two countries with this incident having local support. The war with Iraq in 1980 was a disaster for both countries as they were economically impacted apart from the human and material loss. While it was instigated by the Iraqi leader Saddam Hussain who wanted to exert his influence in the Arab world as well as capture the oil fields, many countries including the west supported him. While Iran was taken aback with the initial attack, they managed to repulse it and hold on in the bloody conflict. A truce came about only in 1988 when it became a stalemate. There were reports of political prisoner executions carried out by the regime in the post war period.

While the transitions after Khomeni were not exactly seamless, the political situation was stable. There were some attempts like that from President Rafsanjani to open the country with the rest of the world but there was little support at home. However, the Iranian nuclear program almost got them to the brink of attacks by Israel and US. Finally, this was settled only in 2015 through the Iranian nuclear deal which was signed in the United Nations.

With the US withdrawing from the nuclear deal in 2018, the country is back to its isolationalist position. There were repeated incidents involving Israel and the US with attacks and assassinations. Hamas which is funded by Iran has been the centre of the dispute with Israel. The 2024 attack by Hamas on an Israeli settlement provoked a crisis in the region. This had led to Iran being almost directly involved in the conflict with Israel. There were missiles fired into the latter which had the protection of the Iron Dome.

Finally, coming to the behavioural pattern has been circumscribed by the history of the country now transitioning to a religious state. This conservative era is reflected in the thought process of the country as it is politically isolated even in the Arab world with all the disputes. There is no doubt that the Iranian have high quality human resources and natural resource wealth. However, their skirmishes with the West especially US and the war with Iraq has seen the economy not reach its potential. The conservative Islamic regime has also sytmied its growth.

In terms of behaviour, the conservative regime reflects the thought process. Hatred towards the west is an obvious behaviour. However, the people are warm and friendly in general towards others. There would be a hint of suspicion to any business dealings.

****

CHAPTER TWENTY-SEVEN

Greece

Known by other names like the Hellenic Republic, it was the cradle of democracy. Its culture and civilization had a profound effect on the globe. Moreover, it produced some of the greatest thinkers, philosophers, scientists, sculptors and painters. To name a few, Socrates, Aristotle, Ptolemy, Plato.

Human habitation in the region is attributable to both the Paleolithic and Mesolithic era which ended by 7000BC. However, agriculture based societies who are believed to have come from the eastern part i.e. Anatolia in the Neolithic era which lasted till the around 3100BC. It was followed by the Bronze age when metal was used for the first time and the period went until 1050BC. The various civilisations that came up during this period were the Cycladic, Minoan, Eutresis and Mycenean. The latter was a warrior aristocracy that is said to have conquered regions such as Crete.

The Ancient Greek period then started with began in 1100 BC until 146 BC. The first phase was the dark age followed by the archaic period starting in 800BC. The former has the nomenclature due to the invasion by the Dorians who had superior weapons. The archaic period saw the expansion of the kingdom as well as development of the city states, the Greek alphabet and literature. Greek arts and democracy flourished with influence of the Persians waning.

The classical period then began in the 5th century BC and first saw the wars with the Persians. The Athenian democracy emerged during this period. They managed to defend themselves in two decisive battles with the city states helping out each other. In the process, they formed the Delian League which was a coalition of the city states for strengthening their military might against the Persian. This was unique and led to the hegemony of Athens which controlled this League. However, an internal conflict emanated and this led to the Peloponnesian war with Sparta taking on the might of Athens. It weakened the latter and let to a truce. However, the second phase of the war began due to a conflict over allies in Sicily and Athenian forces were defeated. The Spartan reign did not last long as other cities rebelled and took the help of the Persian empire which won over Ionia and Cyprus. The Thebans then won a battle with Sparta further weakening it.

With all the internal strife during this period, finally it was Philip II the Macedonian king who unified all the Greek city states. However, the greatest event in this period was the campaign of his son, Alexander the Great who conquered the Persian empire and went all the way upto the shores of India. He managed to establish more than twenty cities including Alexandria in Egypt. His death in 323BC is what ended this period and one of the largest empires in the globe.

This was followed by the Hellenistic period which had a profound influence on the Roman Empire and the western civilization. With the death of the greatest Greek general, there was bound to be rebellions with Athens rising first. However, these were quelled but the Macedon rulers could never keep other uprisings in check despite defeating the Spartans. Philip V tried to unite the Greeks but the Roman empire started eyeing the country ever since they defeated Carthage.

During the 2nd century BC, the Romans occupied the country and made it part of their empire. It was divided into four provinces including Macedonia and eventually were given the same status as Rome. It became part of the Eastern Roman Empire. The Greek culture remained preserved during this period.

With the division of the Roman Empire into the western and eastern region, the Byzantine rule began in the latter around 324AD with its capital at Constantinople. This also elevated the status of Greece as it became an important region of the Eastern Roman Empire. The middle period of the Byzantine empire witnessed attacks from adversaries such as the Persians, Lombards, Avars, Slavs, Arabs and Bulgars. This was a difficult phase for the empire but it slowly recovered. The last phase until 1204 was a period of prosperity and Greek culture too flourished.

The 4th Crusade in 1204 was originally intended to recapture Jerusalem from its Islamic rulers. It planned to set sail from Venice but was joined by forces from many parts of the empire including France. However, the Crusaders got into a political tangle with the Byzantine Empire and eventually ransacked Constantinople and Zara. It was also the result of the animosity between the Venetians and the Byzantine Empire. Even Pope Innocent III was shocked at the brutality of the Crusaders in plundering churches and their treasures. He even ex-communicated them, albeit temporarily. The empire after its capture was divided into three states. This lead to the eventual weakening of the Byzantine empire and its capitulation in 1453 at the hands of the Ottomans.

The weakening of the Byzantine Empire finally led to the occupation by the Ottomans beginning from the 15th century until 1821. They conquered the whole of the country except the Ionian islands which were in the hands of the Venetians. While there was religious freedom, there were tensions too especially with the Greeks who converted to Islam. The Ionian islands had their self-governing Hellenic system intact.

While independence from the Ottomans was declared in 1821, the rulers were driven out only in 1827. This was on account of the combined forces of the British, French and Russians destroying the Ottoman and Egyptian armada. The governor of the First Republic managed to make the country militarily powerful. However, after his assassination, the country was turned into a monarchy by the European powers. The Greeks could not play their geo-political cards well when they decided on expansion to Greek speaking lands. They could not co-ordinate with Russia and were defeated by the British and French. However, they got the Ionian islands from the British and Thessaly from the Ottomans.

The Balkan wars held in 1912-13 were initially a coalition of four Balkan nations Bulgaria, Greece, Montenegro and Serbia as they took on the Ottoman empire and defeated them. They wrested back some territories. However, the second phase was strangely an internecine war as Bulgaria sought to conquer Macedonia and hence faced the wrath of all the others Balkans, Romania and the Ottomans. However, this war catapulted Greece as a victor and enabled it to expand its territory. This included Crete, Epirus, Macedonia and the northern part of the Aegean islands.

World War I saw an internal division since the Greek Emperor was a German sympathizer. This dissension forced the Emperor to abdicate and his son was installed. Despite the wavering stand, the Greeks were beneficiaries of the spoils of the war as they got the territories of the Ottoman's like the city of Izmir and other Greek speaking regions. However, the Turkish nationalists led by Kemal Ataturk overthrew the Ottomans and launched a counteroffensive. They managed to defeat the Greeks and recapture Izmir which was also burnt leading to deaths of Armenians and Greeks. The war from 1919-22 saw the finality with exchange of population of the Orthodox Christians and Muslims. Coupled with the genocide of the Greeks at the hands of the Ottomans, the historian's terms this as an abject surrender by Greece and its dark chapter.

The country was in the forefront of World War II with the installation of a quasi fascist regime of Prime Minister Metaxas. However, they were in the Allies camp and managed to repulse the first attack from Italy in 1940 with the help of British and ANZAC forces. However, with Germany, albeit reluctantly, entering the fray, they could not withstand the second attack. The Nazis overran the country despite stiff opposition with a large loss of paratroopers and it came under occupation. However, many argue that the commitment of the German forces in Greece may have been a critical factor that delayed the Nazi assault on the Soviet Union and changed the course of the war. Even Hitler is said to have blamed his ally, the Italians in not being able to take Greece, as a key factor in the Nazi loss. With the Nazis retreating in front of the Red Army counteroffensive through Romania, the German troops left the country in October 1944 so as not to be cut off. This was the liberation of the country which however suffered immensely. It is estimated that the war cost Greece 8% of its population and more than 2000 villages and towns were razed to the ground.

As of the second World War had not done enough damage to the country, it became a stage in 1944 for a civil war. It was the cold war era and the communist party, the KKE sought to establish control over the country. All the usual suspects like Britain, US, Soviet Union and Yugoslavia jumped into the fray. It was a bitter battle which went on until 1949 in the highlands of northern Greece. It culminated with the NATO bombings and defeat for the communists. The country then aligned itself with the west and its economy grew dramatically until 1970.

However, in 1967 there was a military coup which led to the isolation of the country from the European Union. It was only in 1974 that the monarchy was overthrown and a democratically elected government was installed. The Greek socialist party came to power and dominated the landscape. With the entry back into the EU and funding from the Union, the economy continued to do well.

The 2008 economic recession hit the country and it entered into a debt crisis. While the IMF bailed it out, there was internal resentment due to the harsh austerity measures adopted. It also saw a radical leftist leaning party, the SYRIZA came to power replacing the Socialists in 2015. Subsequently a right leaning New Democratic Party came to power in 2019. The forecasts for the country during the middle of the 2020 decade are rosier than the rest of Europe with expected growth rate of 3%.

The rich history of Greece provides a glimpse of the behavioural pattern of its people. There is no doubt that they are proud of their culture and heritage having produced the greatest of thinkers and philosophers. One of them Socrates had said, *"The only true wisdom is in knowing you know nothing"* which is a reflection of the importance of intellectual pursuit as a trait and got personified in the country. The others like Aristotle, Epicurus and Heraclitus have all brought forth the virtues of reasoning, perseverance and striving for excellence I Greek society. They are also shrewd businessmen and many of the immigrants who settled in the US have done well. Having seen a lot of persecution from the Ottomans, they tend to be conservative as far a religious outlook is concerned. They are quite friendly in their demeanour and believe in establishing long term relationships.

****

Italy

The country which can arguably lay claim to have probably one of the richest heritage with the most expansive Roman empire. This empire personifies the spirit of courage as enunciated by Livy, *"fortune favours the brave"*. It has been a bedrock of culture which is taught in most history books around the world. It also produced some of the greatest scientists and artists.

However, habitation began in this country nearly a million years back. There were traces of people who migrated here during the copper and bronze age. The Nuragic civilization of Sardinia and southern Corsica is said to have come from the 18th century BC to 2nd century AD. This is characterized by the Nuragic towers. The Etrusian civilization took root around the 8th century BC in central Italy. However, they came in conflict with the other civilizations like the Carthagians, Greeks, Romans and Samnites. They lost battles and were finally assimilated into Rome around 500BC.

The Italic people is a generic name for the ethnolinguistic group inhabiting the region like Latins, Osci, Samnites, Umbri and Venetti. There were power struggles among them before the Latins of Rome had the ascendancy and united all of them. Those who came from other regions and settled here were the Celts and the Magna Graecia. The latter were Greeks who settled in Sicily and had an influence on the language and culture of the region.

The Latins were at the epicentre of the Roman empire. Rome was founded in 753BC with successive rule by seven kings. It eventually became a republic in 509BC with a representative assembly, separation of powers and a constitution. One of the key traits that was inculcated during this period was the sense of civic duty as personified by the quote of Cicero, *"There is but one universal rule for making good decisions: to consider the good of the whole community."*

There were a number of tussles with the Gauls, Germanic tribes, Tarentum, Carthage, Macedonian and Selucids but the empire prevailed. It unified the country and through conquests came to dominate the whole of Western Europe, Northern Africa as well as some parts of Eastern Europe and Middle East. It is said to have had naval control over the North Sea, Mediterranean, Atlantic coasts, Red Sea and Black Sea. One of the great rulers was Julius Ceasar who is credited to have conquered the region of Gaul or modern day France. However, he was assassinated in 44BC by his senators. Octavian was another great ruler who defeated the Egyptians in 31BC. Octavian assumed absolute power and ruled the empire for around four decades. Roman Italy was the chief control centre. This was also the golden age of Latin Literature with poets such as Vergil, Horace, Rufus and Ovid. It was also the phase of the conquest of Britain. They also engaged in warfare with the Germanic tribes and the Parthian empire. There were three Jewish revolts too during the period 115-136AD. In 395AD, the empire was divided into the western and eastern part with the former being subjected to increasing raids. It was also the centre of an economic and political crisis. The empire went on till 476AD with the deposing of the last Western emperor Augustulus.

The subsequent Middle Ages were a tumultuous period for the country. First of these was the Gothic wars when the Eastern empire sought to establish hegemony. Using this opportunity of an internal strife, the Lombards, a Germanic tribe took over parts of north Italy ending the Byzantine rule. Based on an appeal of the Papacy, the Franks in 776AD attacked and defeated the Lombards and established the Papal State. Charlemagne was the emperor of the Holy Roman Empire in 800AD. However, on his death there was a succession battle and the country was weakened. The Caliphates took advantage of this and established their rule in places like Sicily in 902 AD.

From the 11th century onwards, there was realignment of power. The Lombards joined together in communes and defeated emperor Barbarossa in 1176. On the other hand, the Normans consolidated their power in the southern part of the country and even drove out the Muslim rulers in Sicily. The 12th and 13th centuries saw the mushrooming of merchant republics like Florence, Genoa, Lucca, Siena and Venice which became financial and commercial centres of the country. There were maritime republics too which came up around this time like Amalfi, Ancona, Gaeta, Noli, Pisa and Ragusa. With all this development, there was significant economic disparity as the south and central parts of the country were much poorer than the rich North.

Italy witnessed the renaissance period during this time. It had a profound impact on architecture, arts, literature, political theory and science. The principle of humanism emanated during this period fuelled also by the migration of Greeks after the fall of Constantinople. The period got a boost in economic development with some of the key centres being Florence, Genoa, Milan and Venice. Venice even became an international financial centre with the first trading of bonds. Italian explorers such as John Cabot, Christopher Columbus, Amerigo Vespucci, Verrazzano and Da Conti discovered new lands. The 14th century also saw wars between the states including with the help of mercenaries from Germany and Switzerland. In the ensuring power struggle Florence, Milan and Venice emerged as the strongest. As far as the seas were concerned, Venice emerged as a maritime power. Thus the entire empire had been fragmented into city states.

There were external invasions too in the 16th century by the French, Spanish, Turks and mercenaries from Germany. Many of the city states bore the brunt and were economically devasted through both destruction of property and payment of debt to the invaders. The Counter Reformation of the 17th century was a Catholic church response to the Protestant Reforms. The Spanish

Hapsburg and subsequently the Austrian Hapsburg took over some of these cities like Milan, Naples and Sicily in the 18th century. However, the war of the Spanish succession and the threat of French hegemony saw alliance between Austria, British, Dutch and some states like Savoy. However, the ensuring warfare really devasted the Italian economy.

At the end of the 18th century, Napoleon attacked Italy and managed to capture most of it ending with the capture of Rome in 1809. Republics were set up with Milan being one of the major ones. Under French rule, they had to pay reparations and provide military support. However, on the positive side, the tricolour was adopted during this period and is even celebrated today. After the defeat of Napolean in 1814 by Russia and other allied powers, the city states came into the possession of Austria, Sardinia and Tuscany. However, this was the beginning of the process of unification of the states.

The unification process began in 1814 with the Italian wars of independence. The uprisings began with the Kingdom of the two Sicilies and Piedmont but they could not defeat the Austrian rulers. The Carbonari or charcoal burners were the first great revolutionaries who were inspired by the French revolution. Mazzini and Garibaldi played a critical role in this movement to unify Italy. The revolutionaries wanted unification under the House of Savoy. The Italian war of independence did not go very well initially in 1848 as Sardinia lost. However, the second war of independence led to the defeat of the Austrians and annexation of Lombardy-Venetia. Garibaldi even tried to get Nice to be part of Italy but could not succeed in 1871. Central Italy became the Papal states which were under the influence of the Catholicism.

The unification also lay bare the disparity between the North and South with the latter having poor governance, difficult conditions of work and high crime rates. A lot of Italians especially from the south emigrated to the US. Moreover, after the kingdom of Italy came into being, it aligned with the Prussians and managed to get some territories from the Austrians like Venice. The unification process went well into World War 1 as the country was enlarged. There was economic disparity with the southern part remaining largely rural and economically impoverished.

The political system of parliamentary democracy was also entrenched at this point of time. However, some of the regimes like that of Depretis were authoritarian while that of Crispi was of an aggressive foreign policy. This was however at the cost of neglecting agriculture wherein there was a breakup of lands and only the landlords were being benefitted. The Giolitte regime from 1901-1914 then initiated some socialist reforms of labour, nationalization, reduction of debt and improvement in infrastructure. However, there was a general strike by the Socialist Party after an incident involving the killing of anti-militarist demonstrators.

After this unification , the country went into the colonial conquest phase by taking lands in Africa and countries along the Mediterranean sea. It started off with Somalia as also a war with Ethiopia in 1895. In 1911, occupation of Libya was attempted which was successful. The Dodocanese islands were taken after the war with the Turks.

In World War 1, Italy sided with the Allied powers and won over Trento and Trieste. However, this was a difficult choice given the affiliation they had with Austria and Germany. The economic condition was also not conducive for the country to take on the brunt of a war. They lost more than half a million soldiers in the war and did not fare well in the fights. The war however led to the collapse of the Austrian Hungarian empire. However, Italy was not given the land promised in the Treaty of London specifically Albania and Dalmatia. The French and Britishers divided all the gains among themselves leaving Italy in the lurch. This was what sowed the seeds of rise of fascism wherein Benito Mussolini took over the reins of power in 1922. Moreover, in 1919, there was support to annex the city of Fiume which was finally undertaken. However, Mussolini's party was initially inclined towards the left and addressed issues of social revolution, proportional representation, women's suffrage and distribution of rural land. The Fascists subtly took over power and Mussolini became authoritarian in his approach suppressing all dissent. He also banked upon the defeat by Ethiopia and restoration of the pride of the Roman empire to solicit support. There were attempts by the Fascist Party to take over Corfu, parts of Albania and Italian speaking parts of France. It was also eyeing Dalmatia and hence did not have good relations with Yugoslavia. It was a hot and cold relationship with the Nazis even at the time Mussolini met Hitler in 1934 since the former was suspicious of German expansionism. However, the turning point was the Italian invasion of Ethiopia in 1935 which led to the international isolation of the country. It was only Germany that supported them and hence Mussolini was forced to ally with Germany and get out of the League of Nations.

Hence when World War II broke out, Italy sided with the Axis powers with Mussolini at the helm of affairs. However, they did not have the same firepower as the Nazis and were not very successful in the campaigns. Their attacks on France, Egypt and Greece ran into rough weather and finally they were defeated. Some gains were made in Slovenia, Dalmatia, Montenegro and Croatia. They had to depend on the Nazi firepower on some fronts to help them out. In the Soviet Union, they lost large number of men as the Red Army counterattacked. Some of the reasons for these setbacks were the poor state of the economy, insufficient equipment and the bombing of Italian cities. The Egyptian campaign was a disaster and the coup de grace was the defeat at El Alamein. Moreover, the Italian resistance movement in 1943 led to the capture of Mussolini, effectively handing over power to Pietro Badoglio as Prime Minister. The Nazis rescued Mussolini but they too were tasting defeat on all fronts as Italy fell to the Allies. Mussolini was tried for treason and hung in 1945 and all the Italian territories were liberated off Nazi rule.

In 1946, the monarchy was abolished and the country became a republic laying the foundation for democratic form of governance. Italy was stripped off all its colonial possessions. They were one of the founding Members of the European Union, NATO and the Group of Six.

It has had a tumultuous period ever since being a republic. The 1950s and 1960s saw tremendous economic boom and raise in standard of living. However, the 1973 oil crisis and the unrest of 1969-70 put paid to hopes. The infrastructure was also improved during this time. The 1970s saw a spate of political violence. In the 1990s, there were extremist attacks by the Sicilian mafia, government debt, excessive corruption and increasing crime rate. The governance ever since has been one of concern as the economic growth has been lukewarm. With the growing immigration issues, the centre right coalition has been in power since 2022 under Giorgia Melloni.

A country with a rich history and the Roman Empire that virtually ruled Europe, it lost all this grandeur in the middle ages as the empire split and external invasions occurred. The concept of city states very similar to Greece emanated from this civilization. The Renaissance brought out the best of its arts, culture, scientific discoveries and explorations. However, the attacks by the Spanish, Austrians, Arabs and eventually Napoleon reduced the country to the city states trying to survive. The unification process managed to ensure the amalgamation of the city states but it was still under pressure. Despite being on the winning side of World War 1, the inability to get the desired territories sowed the seeds of fascism. World War II was a disaster both in terms of choosing the wrong side but of the economic devastation. The North South divide underscores the deep internal social tensions in the country. The economic revival has not been commensurate as that of the rest of Europe and with the immigration issue cropping up, the right wing parties have got a foothold.

All in all, it is a case of a rich history somehow not being carried over after the middle ages. The behaviour is general more boisterous and effusive than others. However, social inequality has led to high crime rates. The tradition of being merchants has made them good business particularly in the commercial centres of the north. One can expect them not to be particularly sophisticated in their approach to commercial dealings. As one Italian proverb goes *"Patience is bitter, but its fruit is sweet."* Hence, they could curb their natural trait of spontaneity when doing business deals.

****

CHAPTER TWENTY-NINE

Turks

Assyrian clay tablets were found in the region believed to be of period around 2000BC. However, the Turkic people are believed to have lived in the region from the 6th century BC onwards. There were on the periphery of the Xiongnu confederation that came up in 200 BC. This was under the control of the Han dynasty of China.

The Asian part of the country in the east was Anatolia while the European part was known as Thrace. While the former had a number of states like Phyrgia and Lydia; the latter was inhabited by the Thracian tribes. They were finally overrun by the Achaemenid Persian Empire. There were a number of revolts which were suppressed by the Empire.

On the other hand, Thrace also saw the defeat of the Persian empire and it came under the Odrysian Kingdom. However, the region eventually was conquered by the Kingdom of Macedon.

However, the Persians were driven out of the region by Alexander the Great as the Greeks exerted their influence in the region during 330BC. It became part of the Seleucid Empire under which Anatolia came. However, there were skirmishes with the Gauls, Pergamon, Pontus and Egypt. The region also saw the pervasive influence of Hellenistic culture.

A disastrous battle with the Roman empire ensued resulting in the Seleucids giving up Anatolia in 188BC. It was during this period that Constantinople came up. The Roman empire gave a lot of autonomy to the region. It eventually was part of the eastern part of the empire and was known as the Byzantine Empire. It was the period when the Gokturks came up and ruled the region. They established provinces known as Khanates and also began the Turkic script. The Byzantines had frequent battles with the Sassanids over the territory which led to considerable weakening of the forces during the 7th century AD. It set the ground for the invasion, first by the establishment of the Seljuk Empire. The Seljuks who owe their origin in Turkmenisation finally succumbed to the Mongol invasion.

The Ottomans then expanded their base to cover Anatolia with clashes with the Byzantine Empire. These led to the eventual fall of Constantinople to the Ottoman Empire in 1453. The power of the Ottoman's peaked during the reign of Suleiman during the 16th century. They had wars with the Holy Roman and Persian Empires. Their maritime prowess was vindicated by the battles with the Portuguese to control merchant routes as well as influence in South East Asia. However, the Ottoman-Habsburg wars weakened them and they lost most of these territories in South and East Europe. Anatolia was multicultural at that point of time. However, the increased exodus of Muslims from the lost territories also led to an internal policy of Turkification and violence against the Greeks and Armenians.

The Ottomans sided with Germany as Central powers in World War 1 and were eventually defeated. They had defended the Dardanelles Strait and even scored decisive wins over the British forces. However, they were overrun in the Caucuses by the Russians. It was during their period that the Armenian genocide was carried out. Post war, the empire was divided and the victors took the spoils.

The Turkish National Movement in 1920 led to the establishment of a Republican State. The Sultanate was abolished in 1922 formally ending the Ottoman monarchy. The Treaty of Lausanne led to the withdrawal of the Allied troops and recognition of the Turkish Republic in 1923. The reforms by Kemal Ataturk made the country a nation state with key ones being the abolition of the caliphate as well as the sharia, bestowing rights of women, adoption of European legal systems, alphabets based on Latin system, introduction of the Gregorian calendar and the metric system as well a five year industrial plan.

Its diplomatic finesse came to the front during the second World War. While initially cosying upto Britain and seeking its protection from any German attack, it continued to trade with the latter. It promised the Allies to enter into the war. When German defeat was imminent it make a shambolic severing of ties with the country and even entered into a war with Germany and Italy. This move enabled it to join the United Nations.

In the post war era, the relations with the Soviet Union went into a spin and it took the side of the western powers in the cold war. It served the latter's interest to contain the communist influence in the Mediterranean participated in the Korean war against the north. This also earned it a NATO membership in 1952. Its first real military campaign was in Cyprus against the Greek where it occupied one part of the island and declared a separate republic in the north.

The country had seen a number of coups and unrests. However, it managed to have greater political stability after the liberalization of the economy in 1980. President Erdogan came after the Presidential election of 2014. He has ruled the country with an iron hand. He has played the diplomatic card well by maintaining close relations with the western powers as well as China. The country has gone into manufacturing of military hardware including drones. These have played decisive roles in some global disputes such as Armenia-Azerbaijan wherein it supplied the latter with hardware which was decisive in the battle over Nagorno Karabakh in 2022. It has also supplied weapons to Pakistan to keep its borders with India and Afghanistan on a knife's edge. In the Russia Ukraine conflict, they supplied weapons to the latter. However, when NATO was toying with the idea of expanding to include Sweden and Finland as a riposte to Russia, it opposed the entry of the former ostensibly citing its immigration policies. This won it favour with the Islamic world. It has also been cozying up to the China playing a smart move keeping everyone including the NATO on the tenterhooks. This shows their clever diplomatic maneuvering as and when the circumstances demand.

The Turks are warm and friendly people and believe in a lot of socializing. But ironically, history has taught them to wary of outsiders. They would hence straddle positions depending on the political climate. With significant population in many European countries, they do exert a marginal influence there. While post World War 1, the country undertook reforms which pushed it outside the powers of an theocratic state, the undercurrents of fundamentalism run deep, especially in the eastern part of the country. Hence, religion plays a crucial role in their approach to the world.

****

CHAPTER THIRTY

Summary

From all the literature above, it is clear that from the history of a nation, it is possible to gauge the behaviourial pattern of its people. There are definitely a lot of polito-geographical factors that have influenced this behaviour. Some of these include the climatic conditions to the topography of the nation. As Peter Gabriel said, *"As many an architect will tell you, human behavior changes according to the environment."*

Living in an island is another aspect of the response of the people. Then landlocked countries emanate the feeling of insecurity which also manifests in the behaviour of the denizens. Large nations on the other hand could have both an outward looking expansionist tendences or may be troubled by regional strifes emanating from the diversities. Some nations despite not being large have evolved to be regional powerhouses. One could say that the leadership qualities are ingrained in them and they also have economic clout. The developing countries beset with possibly a rich history but the subsequent draining of all that wealth in the colonial rule period calls for a separate set of behavioural patterns. Finally, those with a rich ancient civilization which subsequently disintegrated and subject to a lot of invasions has seen a different mindset.

The type of rule ranging from democratic to autocratic would also influence how citizens respond to particular situations. The former could see a lot of dissenting voices and may stymie decision making. On one end of the spectrum is the country which epitomizes free speech, the United States where dissensions are tolerated and people are free to speak their mind. On the other end of the spectrum are countries like North Korea where people are brainwashed to worship their leaders right from school and tutored to be suspicious of all foreigners. The behaviour would be vastly different in both.

While we have already summarized the behavioural pattern of the countries in the respective chapters, let us not take a look at these patterns and the strategy to be adopted to deal with these countries

1. **Britain:**

i. It is important to put them in their place from the lofty pedestal from which they would try to interact including pontification. Stiff upper lip is the apt behavioural trait that has percolated down from the colonial period. One way is to be brash and give them back in equal measure on the demands they make. Indirect references to the colonial period of infamy could be a good means.

ii. Be careful of how they play with words, especially when they can couple it with a good sense of humour too. After all they gloat over the Kings tongue and believe it to be the greatest gift of theirs to mankind. It is important not to get trapped in this and one must analyse what they say and what they actually mean.

iii. Always remember that beneath the veil of the gentlemanly behaviour, they have a mercantilist mindset. So it is money that finally matter irrespective of the means. Interact with them based on this premise and learn to cut beneath this false cloak of sophistication.

iv. Racist tendencies percolate quite deep, not surprisingly, based on their colonial past. Learn to confront it upfront.

v. Being the masters of divide and rule, expect them to use this tactic effectively in business deals. They could get in touch with stakeholders who may harbour some resentment and try to play this card. They would also try to be in touch with third parties to put pressure.

vi. They are capable of lying through mis-interpretation of words in order to achieve this objective. One way is to open up multiple channels of communication within the system. They could then feed the other channels with misinformation in order to extract some concessions and use this for fulfilment of the objective.

1. **France**

i. Communication is about sweet talk and beating around the bush before coming to the point. It is not businesslike and one would need to adapt to this method and not reveal too much in the conversations. They would be smart in eliciting information.

ii. Given their pride for the French culture and language, it maybe prudent to strike a conversation on that aspect. The richness of the renaissance period may also be a good point for initiating conversation.

iii. The colonial past has a chequered history and they exploited the economic resources of their colonies and even imposed the culture. Hence, they would be good at business deals and one must be wary on this front since it is coupled with the art of talking around in circles.

iv. There is an element of socialist thinking in politics and hence labour and human rights are top of their agenda. Radical capitalist ideas may not seep in deep during conversations.

v. They are very critical of themselves and one must not be gullible to reciprocate this. It could be used as a means of seeking information.

vi. Even if they do not have much knowledge of cultures beyond Europe, have a good habit of reading up. Hence, be prepared that they may have adequate information on your culture and behaviour.

3. New Zealand

i. The small island spirit evokes the concept of being self-sustaining without dependency on others. Hence, their initial reaction would be reluctance to be part of broader coalition of countries and would need to be given that extra coaxing.

ii. While they would like to believe that they have integrated the indigenous Maoris in the mainstream, the situation is not that rosy given the historical baggage of the Treaty of Waitangi which was not implemented in spirit and substance. Basically, all the land was usurped. Hence, one can expect a tinge of racism or arrogance towards the indigenous people despite the overt display of inclusivity. One can always broach the subject of implementation of the Treaty of Waitangi as it would be sore point.

iii. While there is a pride about their culture, this also manifests in the form of a superiority complex. This could again resurface elements of racism when dealing with others specially developing countries. One must be prepared for this.

iv. There would be a tendency to be circumspect when dealing with large nations such as their neighbours Australia. It is the small island syndrome which also persisted during the time of the decision to join the Federation.

4. Japan

i. In business dealings it is necessary to establish relationships over a long phase of interaction. Japanese take their own time since they do a lot of consultations and checks. They undertake due diligence and hence one must be careful about what is spoken or committed.

ii. As a result of the due diligence, their decision making can be slow and sometimes frustrating. One must avoid showing anger or direct confrontation since this is not considered a good trait. Patience is a virtue that is admired.

iii. Expect racist behaviour stemming from the colonial past and the period of the Takugawa shogunate. However, this would not be overt and gets masked in the politeness and courtesy that they show. But internally, this is seething.

iv. In business dealings, expect them to have large teams including youngsters on probation. They believe in building up teams and do a meticulous homework on their counterparts. It is important not to be overwhelmed by these numbers or the information they have on you.

v. Decision making being slow should not be an irritant. It is important to play out this time without being irritated or expressing displeasure.

vi. They are very keen on punctuality and hence one must avoid being late for meetings or appointments.

5. **Switzerland**

i. Money is the primary driver in their psyche and any business deals would have to take this into account. They are shrewd businessmen and so one needs to be careful in transactions.

ii. Decision making can be fast and business like. One doesn't have to invest time and resources in relationship building. So there is no purpose of beating around the bush.

iii. Racism does exist as they even consider the other parts of Europe a notch below their own development. So expect this to surface during conversations. One way of giving it back is to remind them of their infamous role in WWII where they provided monetary support to the Nazis in lieu of buying peace.

iv. They are adept at playing the divide and rule card given their history of dealing with large empires across the borders. Be cautious of this strategy with money being the root mechanism for achieving this objective.

6. **Mongolia**

i. Culture and religion are deeply ingrained and hence one must respect all this in the interactions. The trust and respect have to be earned and one cannot adopt an upfront *"coming to the point"* tactic.

ii. Having sought Russian help to save them from Chinese invasion, the influence of the former and the communist regime is profound. Hence, in business dealings, one cannot expect a business like capitalist approach.

iii. With an inward looking policy, there could be some caution and suspicion towards foreigners. The fear is of exploitation of resources.

7. Afghanistan

i. It was historically a trading nation and hence they have a good business sense. However, the portfolio of traded products is limited given the accessibility of the nation. Hence, don't expect them to conversant with the modern nuances of trade.

ii. Fundamentalism is at the root of the Taliban which is in power. Therefore, one cannot expect them to respect liberal views or freedom of speech. Religious bigotry also exists in deep measure. One must be careful on the choice of words and be circumspect when dealing with this emotive issue..

iii. The attitude towards women is archaic and hence there would be less receptivity on topics such as equality for women. It would be better not to broach this subject.

iv. The people are by and large warm and hospitable provided you do not broach sensitive topics. Hence, it would be important to build up relationships.

8. China

i. They are possibly the shrewdest businessmen in the globe and one needs to be at the peak of concentration when doing business deals. They would do all the homework and background checks. One must be prepared for the eventuality of them having adequate information on the counterparty.

ii. They would come with mandates and if the brief exceeds that, no one would dare take a decision without consent of the superiors. There is little flexibility for negotiators to exceed their briefs since consequences can be severe. One must therefore not be impatient if the team cannot take decisions at the spur of the moment.

iii. There is an air of suspicion and mistrust towards outsiders, probably stemming from the communist regime. Hence, one must be careful as to what one says and even speaks in private conversations. It is not out of context that the rooms could be bugged or conversations could be tapped, even in public transport.

iv. In normal conversations, one would notice the hesitation to be open about matters. It is a fall out of the regime under which they operate. Therefore, it would take time to forge relationships after a level of comfort has been established. Once again there is virtue in being patient and tenacious.

v. If one shares borders or sea, there is a need to be doubly cautious as the land grabbing genes are ingrained in the communist party. The only way is to enhance the military might to prevent any incursions on some pretext or the other. One cannot afford to drop any guard against them especially when they have become so powerful militarily.

vi. Moolah is the big weapon that they have and this can be used to play the divide and rule policy. Geopolitical alignments would be undertaken on this pretext and one may need to counter it through coalition building on their own.

9. **Australia**

i. The White Australia Policy, though annulled is still reflected in the behavioral mindset of the people. There is a big tinge of racism especially towards non-whites and this has been felt by many expats. While it may not be overt, the undercurrents are visible. One would therefore have to be prepared for this.

ii. The treatment of the Aborigines is another major issue in the country. While discrimination does not exist on paper, they have not been economically integrated into mainstream society and have been made dependent on the doles given by the government. Such freebees have more disastrous consequences.

iii. On the business front, the general demeanour is more relaxed than the US or European counterparts. Hence, one can expect such meetings to be more cordial without the pressure cooker environment.

iv. Relationships are built over long term and over social gatherings. They are generally fun loving people and one would need to invest time in building confidence.

10. Canada

i. Given the unique combination of the British and French influence, the level of trust has to moderated and one must not take their word at face value in meetings. It is a concoction of the British still upper lip and French obfuscation.

ii. One can expect a level of racism when dealing with other cultures. While they were not colonial powers, the interaction with immigrants has been one of the factors. Many a time, they may not mince their words in expressing this displeasure.

iii. The treatment and integration of the indigenous people has also left a lot to be desired. The discriminatory attitude still persists in dealing with them.

iv. The work culture is generally more relaxed especially when compared their southern neighbour. One need not be under pressure to make quick decisions. Nevertheless, a brash to the point statement is not taken as overtly offensive since there is influence of the US ethics too.

v. They could go to any extent to placate their constituencies and have known to harbour, fund and encourage secessionist elements. The garb of free speech is given as justification for all this.

vi. They are also apt at using the policy of divide and rule. Hence, expect them to be in touch with all players of the counterparties to create an internal rift.

vii. The relationship with US has been hot and cold. The historical mistrust coupled with the scale of development of the neighbour are factors for this attitude.

11. United States

i. Given their superpower status, the negotiators can be blunt. The tone can also be arrogant and in some cases almost a threat of talking to superiors in the system. It may be a good tactic to give it back to them in equal measure in such circumstances.

ii. They are more business like i.e. style of being to the point rather than beating around the bush. This also leads to faster decision making.

iii. The virtues of punctuality and discipline are important in any business deals with them.

iv. Racism exists given the background of the treatment of the Afro-Americans and Hispanics. Therefore, expect some elements of it. However, the country has evolved into being one of the most tolerant ones despite the undercurrents.

v. Conversations with them can be free wheeling as they encourage new ideas and out of the box thinking. This is ingrained in their education system which attracts some of the best talent in the world.

12. Russia

i. The citizens are warm and friendly and one needs to build relationships with them over social gatherings.

ii. The communist hangover still persists despite perestroika. Hence, one could expect some introvert and suspicious behaviour during business discussions.

iii. They are fiercely patriotic and one must be use in this to converse on the rich Russian history and culture. Reference to their role in the World War II could be important to build up confidence.

iv. Expect decision making to be slow and based on directives from above. The State control is tight and hence mandates would not be easily available.

v. One must expect some skepticism from the western world especially in the present scenario of the conflict with Ukraine where NATO has openly supported the latter.

vi. The power of the oligarchs is sometimes more than the government officials themselves. Hence, it would not be surprising that some representatives of these oligarchs may occupy key positions in government and may be negotiating on their behalf.

vii. They are smart businessmen and have good negotiating skills.

13. Singapore

i. Given the economic development of the country, one can expect a degree of arrogance from then in business dealings especially from developing countries. The strategy is to hold one's own in such circumstances and probably give it back.

ii. In the ASEAN, they have learnt the art of navigating and throwing their weight around. The economic muscle has been smartly flexed with funding carried out to keep the others, albeit the big ASEAN economies too under control. Therefore, in the ASEAN context if one needs to get things moving, it is important to engage with this island country.

iii. Discipline has been ingrained in them and has been the chief factor for their economic growth. Hence, punctuality, courtesy and proper dress code despite the heat are important when dealing with them.

iv. They believe in coming to the point and not beating around the bush. Hence, they could show impatience and anger if one uses the latter tactic.

v. The small island mentality does surface and there is a sense of maintaining adequate security. The community bonding is also closer and there is a move towards living a sustainable lifestyle.

14. Germany

i. The historical baggage of World War II has definitely kept some racist tendencies alive but it is not obvious in the interactions. The economic prosperity and immigration issues have fuelled this trait. One must be cognizant of it.

ii. In business, they are forthright and to the point. They do not like to dilly dally or talk in a convulated manner. This directness could be interpreted as being rude and blunt.

iii. They embrace good work ethics like being punctual, efficient, orderly, commitment, reliability and adherence to rules and regulations.

iv. While committed to work, they keep adequate time for leisure and believe in spending quality time with family and relatives. Hence, one cannot intrude into this space with business matters.

15. South Africa

i. The cultural diversity manifests variations in behaviour ranging from racism on account of the apartheid policy of yore as well as compassion due to the multicultural society and the principle of ubuntu. Hence, one would need to frame a response accordingly.

ii. With a difficult history, they have a lot of courage and determination to take on adversities of life. Hence, one can expect them to be resilient in tricky situations.

iii. However, they are by and large warm and friendly people. One would need to build a long term relationship with them.

16. **Brazil**

   i. They have a good sense of business as well as work ethics on account of which it is the largest economy in the region.
  ii. Social inequality persists in the large cities and with many living in slums in the large cities, racist tendencies exist.
 iii. The people are resourceful and adaptable which facilitates exploring out of the box solutions to complex business problems. Hence it facilitates commercial interactions.
  iv. There is emphasis on societal bonding and interactions which is the basis of building relationships. Hence it is important to invest in such interactions to develop the level of trust.

17. **Egypt**

   i. The people are hospitable and warm believing in building up long term relationship. Hence it is important to invest in building up such relationship.
  ii. As they use a lot of body language and expressions, it is important to reciprocate that and show the apt level of engagement and receptivity. This is useful in building relationships too.
 iii. In business deals, they believe in being direct while being expressive. This could be interpreted as being rude. Hence, it is better not to beat around the bush when negotiating with them.
  iv. However, they may hesitate to openly say "*no*" and could sugar coat rejections. One should read into such language.
   v. They have strong work ethics in terms of punctuality, formal dressing up, courtesy and respect. It is important to reciprocate these so as to build up a good rapport.
  vi. It would be a good strategy to discuss the rich history and culture of the country in conversations. They are immensely proud of that given that they had one of the earliest civilisations in the world.

18. Iran

i. Post revolution, the country has been in a phase of diplomatic isolation and this has been reflected in the thought process. Hence, one could be looked at with a lot of suspicion in business dealings due to the conservative inward looking society.

ii. One must also be careful about business deals in the light of the US and consequently western sanctions. It is important to get a legal opinion on the feasibility of the deal as well as the long term implications on relationship with other countries.

iii. However, Iranians generally are warm and hospitable people and like to build up long term relations. Hence, it is important to invest in building up that trust during meeting.

iv. They are good negotiators and the process can get stretched. However, patience is the virtue in such cases.

v. They are proud of their Persian culture and heritage. Make it a point to broach it in the discussions since it would provide an opening for building a good relationship.

vi. One can expect some fundamentalist views give the Islamic revolution. One has to tread carefully on that including on subjects like women's rights.

19. Greece

i. They are shrewd businessmen with many of the immigrants who went to the US having done well. Therefore, one must be prepared well in any business dealings.

ii. Greeks would prefer coming straight to the point and discuss the core issues. It is not advisable to beat around the bush when dealing with them.

iii. They are very expressive in nature and this is a trait that must not be construed as being brash. One must respond in a calm and collected manner.

iv. Work ethics are important in terms of punctuality, dress sense, courtesy and respect.

v. One can play the cultural card since it has been one of the cradles of arts and culture. The Greeks are proud of their heritage and history.

20. Italy

i. With the history of being merchants and traders, they are smart businessmen. One would need to negotiate hard with them.
ii. They would look at the gains for them in any deal. This must be clearly explained rather than having a convoluted conversation.
iii. They have a good social life and like to engage in conversation on it, even in a business context. Hence, one would need to build up a long term relationship through social engagements.
iv. They are boisterous and expressive which could also hinge on being perceived as aggression. However, this is a natural trait and one must be prepared for it.
v. The north south economic divide and the immigration problems have led to elements of racism seeping in. Therefore, one must be aware that far leaning rightist views could be a possibility during conversations.

21. Turks

i. They are warm and social people who believe in long and engaging conversations. Thus there is a need to reciprocate while engaging in business deals.
ii. However, history has taught them to tow a delicate diplomatic line. Hence, they would be wary of countries with whom they don't have good political relations. For one, there would always be the skepticism towards the western world despite being closely integrated with the latter.
iii. They have a good negotiating skill and have a history of being traders in the region.
iv. While it may be a modern state, the head of fundamentalism could rear up in discussions and hence one must be careful

while striking a conversation on religious or political issues.

As discussed earlier, these are broad behavioural traits. One cannot bracket each and every citizen of that nation into that silo. After all with the liberal immigration policy of many nations, there has been a significant change in the demographics of many nations It is of course a different matter that in certain cases, the immigrants show a greater degree of loyalty to the nation than the original denizens. One can't blame them entirely, after all it is the art of survival. Moreover, some of the traits have got modified on account of the immigration itself. It has moulded the behaviour of people towards others including the immigrants.

The books seeks to dwell into how the historical evolution of a country can be used to gauge its behavioural traits. However, one cannot slot each and every person of a nation into a standard list of traits. There could be variations depending on the type of global exposure to other cultures, upbringing, nature of work, economic as well as social status etc. Nevertheless, it would provide a tool that prepares us for interactions, specifically commercial, with citizens of these nations. It is better to be cognizant of all this for the interaction and its outcome to be productive and possibly a win-win for both sides. As Lao Tzu said, "*Knowing others is intelligence; knowing yourself is wisdom*".

****